PARDON *the* INSPIRATION

Devotions for Sports Fans

Al Sturgeon

CENTERFIELD PUBLISHING
Ocean Springs, MS

P.O. Box 272
Ocean Springs, MS 39566-0272
www.centerfieldpublishing.com
Email:centerfieldpub@aol.com

First printing 2005.

ISBN 0-9763924-0-2
Library of Congress Control Number: 2004099182

Cover and Interior Design: Laurie Burke
www.subtext.ca

To my Dad,
who shared with me his love of sports,
and without knowing it, taught me of God.

"This book will be a blessing to any sports fan. I especially liked the manner in which sports lessons are related to life lessons. I would recommend this book to any fan, coach, or athlete." ❖ *Rod Barnes, Men's Basketball Coach, Ole Miss*

"Being from a professional sports background, I found many truths in the stories you share—and being a Christian, I found many truths in their life applications. Your stories show the heart, discipline, and focus it takes to be successful in sports as well as Christian living. Thanks for compiling a book that reminds us what real victory is all about." ❖ *Steve Freeman, NFL Defensive Back 1975-1987, NFL Official 2000-present*

"What a great book! I thought it was outstanding. I plan to use it for my early morning devotionals with my coaching staff. It really made me think of old friends, parents, and overall brought back a bunch of memories." ❖ *Gary Gaines, Head Football Coach, Abilene Christian University (whose story was popularized by the best-selling book and hit movie,* Friday Night Lights.*)*

"This book is a treasure that will tug at the heartstrings of any sports fan as it did mine. Likewise, it will serve the same purpose for anyone looking for an inspiring daily devotional. I plan to make *Pardon the Inspiration* available to my three children and seven grandchildren with the hope that they will receive the same enjoyment and motivation as I did." ❖ *Bailey Howell, NBA 12 years, Naismith Basketball Hall of Fame*

"Have I ever got a deal for you! Al Sturgeon has put together the great gap filler! Gap filler? Sure, that 'what shall I do while I'm waiting?' mixture that keeps us from wasting valuable time. *Pardon the Inspiration* is going to come in mighty handy for all Cub fans in August and September. Tiger might want to check out a couple of the *Inspirations* while he waits in the locker room for Vijay and Phil to finish the 18th. Lance may find his generosity gaining speed as he drops copies of *Pardon* for all those cyclers who annually lag behind. What should Texas fans do while OU plays in the Orange Bowl? Read Al. If you like sports ... or if you know someone who is a sports widow ... you may want to get extra copies of *Pardon the Inspiration* now. Not only is it a great gap filler, it is the perfect stocking stuffer for whatever holiday you support." ❖ *Terry Rush, Minister for the Memorial Drive Church of Christ, and author of* Voice of Silver, Heart of Gold *(a tribute to broadcaster Jack Buck)*

"

First of all, I must thank my beautiful wife and daughters—Jody, Erica and Hillary. Thank you for putting up with my many ideas and the hours they end up consuming, and also for letting me watch Sunday Night Baseball when you'd all rather be watching something else. Thank you for your love most of all, which is more valuable to me than you realize.

Deep thanks goes out to DeJon Redd for his editing advice and his friendship through our common loves of both God and sport.

And thanks as well to CJ Hughes, a true artist, for his work for my business as well as permission to use his caricature of me. The subject was ugly, but the artwork outstanding.

Special thanks to Rod Barnes, Steve Freeman, Gary Gaines, Bailey Howell and Terry Rush, for their comments and valuable time. Most especially, thank you to George Kell for taking the time to write a five-page letter to me longhand on Hall-of-Fame stationery despite his deteriorating health. Mr. Kell is a Hall-of-Famer in the ways that matter most.

Thank you to the Ocean Springs Church of Christ for not only putting up with a seemingly endless string of sports analogies from the pulpit, but also for giving me the opportunity to "coach" there in the first place.

Thanks to all the people spread around the globe that read my email devotionals and encouraged my habit. To those who kept encouraging me to write a devotional book, let me say: At first, I was flattered. Later, I was annoyed. Now, after all is said and done, I'm deeply grateful for all your prompting (especially you, John Dobbs).

I also offer great thanks to all my former coaches, teammates, and opponents who taught me the lessons of sport in the most literal ways as well as all the friends and family who shared with me the fun of being sports fans.

But most of all, I offer my thanks to God—for everything that matters.

Contents

Introduction 1

Spring 3

Week 1 Spring Training 7
Week 2 Golf Miracles 10
Week 3 March Madness 13
Week 4 Opening Day 16
Week 5 The Distance Runner 19
Week 6 The Final Four 22
Week 7 Field of Dreams 25
Week 8 An Amazing Shot 28
Week 9 Obstacles 31
Week 10 The Splendid Splinter 33
Week 11 Extreme Sports 36
Week 12 The NBA Finals 39
Week 13 Stealing Bases 42

Summer 45

Week 14 Fishing Trips 49
Week 15 Summer of '79 52
Week 16 How You Play the Game 55
Week 17 The Minor Leagues 58
Week 18 Special Olympics. 61
Week 19 Radio Baseball 64
Week 20 The Pole Vault 67
Week 21 Fifty-Six 70
Week 22 The Summer Olympics 73
Week 23 Clutch Hitters 76
Week 24 The Stalkers. 79
Week 25 That's a Winner! 82
Week 26 Lance Armstrong 85

Fall 89

Week 27 Backyards 93
Week 28 Church Softball 96
Week 29 Team Loyalty 99
Week 30 Coach Boone 102
Week 31 Unexpected Success 105
Week 32 Y.M.C.A. 108
Week 33 Loneliness. 111
Week 34 The Transfer Principle. 114
Week 35 Playing With Pain 117
Week 36 Blind Bowling 120
Week 37 Game Seven 123
Week 38 Revenge 125
Week 39 Tiger Bait 127

Winter 131

Week 40 Sid 135
Week 41 Fantasy Sports 138
Week 42 Pride 141
Week 43 The Intimidator 144
Week 44 The Streak. 147
Week 45 The Senior Bowl 150
Week 46 Sports Psychology 153
Week 47 Dillon's Hero 156
Week 48 The NFL Experience. 159
Week 49 The Winter Olympics 162
Week 50 Jarrod 165
Week 51 Super Bowl Hero. 168
Week 52 The Brothers of the Barbecue 171

Afterword 175
Resources 177
About the Author 181

Introduction

I am a preacher who loves sports. For some, the very thought of spiritual conversation is an immediate turn-off. For others, the belief exists that those who engage in passionate sports talk have the intellectual depth of Astroturf. I can't imagine what those who feel both ways think about me.

But there are others. There are others who believe in a God that loves the world, and that recognizing Him is a good thing. And there are still others who can't make it through a day without watching ESPN, reading the sports page, and checking their fantasy teams. And for those who represent both ...

You're really going to like this book.

I love days when I make it home in time to catch *Pardon the Interruption* on ESPN. It has got to be my favorite show. Hosts, Tony Kornheiser and Michael Wilbon, have the impressive ability to knock down every topic in the sports world in thirty minutes while running through emotions ranging from the hilariously insane to the seriously profound. They scream, laugh, and argue the whole way through. At the end, they find out where they screwed up, and every single day Kornheiser signs off with his familiar phrase, " ... we'll try to do better next time."

That's this book in a nutshell.

We, too, will cover a lot of ground in a short amount of time. I make no claims to write grand dissertations of theology. Instead, I just like to notice God wherever I happen to see Him, and in this book, I notice Him all over the world of sports. I discovered God at spring training and on a golf course; on television and at the gym; at a football stadium and at the bowling alley. I'm beginning to believe He just might be everywhere!

And like my favorite show, we'll laugh and we'll cry and we'll disagree all along the way. One of my favorite things about watching *PTI* is that Kornheiser and Wilbon typify sports buddies—guys that can just tear into one another, but in the end, do so with a slight smile knowing they will forever be friends. I love that. So as I notice God along my path in this book, I can just about guarantee you'll find lots of laughs, shed a few tears, and even be convinced ever so often that I'm full of it. But we'll have fun anyway. And we'll still be on the same side.

Yogi Berra taught us the philosophical truth, "It ain't over 'til it's over." To the great delight of sports fans, and to the tragic horror of those married to them, sports never do end. This wonderful fact is how you coax Cubs fans down off the ledge every September. There really is always next year, and one season leads straight into another.

My attempt to notice God through the world of sports reflects that design. It all begins in the spring when the grass is green, and it comes to its cold end in the winter. But hope springs eternal in the heart of the sports fan, and more appropriately in the heart of those who believe in God.

So do your best with the trivia, laugh at the funny parts, cry at the emotional ones, and stop to think when a lesson hits home. Believe it or not—finally—a book was written just for you.

I'll try to do better next time.

Al Sturgeon
Summer 2004

SPRING

It all begins in the spring.

The rookies and the veterans; the dreamers and the legends. They all report to the same warm towns in Florida and Arizona to stretch in green grass under an early sun. The old men come out to watch and swap stories of days gone by, some of which are true. They mow the fields, water the base paths, draw chalk lines, and begin the countdown to Opening Day.

And every spring football coaches drape their whistles over their necks and announce the beginning of off-season practice. Young men emerge from the weight rooms and that horrible month without football following the Super Bowl, ready to make contact. In shorts and t-shirts, they strap on their helmets and lace up their cleats, and for a moment frozen in time, tense every muscle for that first whistle of spring.

The Madness comes in spring, too. Brackets are copied, completed, and then destroyed a scant seven days after Selection Sunday. On the court, dreams are both realized and crushed in a matter of moments when last-second shots unleash pandemonium on only one side of the arena. The nets come down. Luther Vandross sings, "One Shining Moment."

Lord Stanley brings out his prized trophy in the spring as well, the most famous thirty-five pounds in all of sports. North American men bleed through the winter dreaming of hoisting it high above their heads on a victorious lap around the ice and having their name forever engraved on the silver chalice. It has traveled for a full year each spring. At playoff time, most players feel it needs a new home.

Augusta National assumes attention in the spring, too. The legends are chauffeured into Georgia, while the hopefuls drive themselves. Groundskeepers prepare Amen Corner for its coming flurry of activity, and dry cleaners prepare several sizes of green jackets for the next champion. The players appear on cue among the live oaks, magnolias, and pine trees, all vying for a prestigious spot in a rich history.

The clay courts of Paris play host to the world each spring. Since 1925, France has invited the world to Roland-Garros stadium to declare the best tennis players in the world, and every year the world has come to watch. Fans of tennis on clay exult.

Louisville in the spring is time for the Derby. The race for the elusive Triple Crown begins here every year at Churchill Downs, where thousands of fans witness breathtaking three-year-old thoroughbreds go at it for one and a quarter miles in the thrilling run for the roses. The Preakness and Belmont eagerly wait their turn. They all race in the spring.

But spring means more than Grapefruit leagues and two-a-days. More than Final Fours and Stanley Cups. More than green jackets and Parisian clay courts. Even more than race tracks for thoroughbreds.

Spring finds it's true meaning in the backyard. In games of catch. In H-O-R-S-E in the driveway. In a family game of touch football. In pulling out the old set of golf clubs. All, of course, within the charcoaled aroma of the barbecue grill.

That is what spring is really all about. The rest is compelling periphery.

Yes, it all begins in the spring.

When life is good.

Week 1: Spring Training

trivia

Q: Which MLB team has the all-time Spring Training attendance record for one year?

"People ask me what I do in the winter when there's no baseball. I'll tell you what I do. I stare out the window and wait for spring."—Rogers Hornsby

What I'll do for my daughter.

Fifty-four hours, thirteen hundred miles, two spring training baseball games, and one mystery dinner theater—all for Erica's sixteenth birthday. Our whirlwind trip to central Florida happened to dodge the rain showers and turn out like a tailor-made 6-4-3 double play. In the middle of it all, however, I found a special moment for me, too.

We were in Winter Haven, Florida, on a Tuesday afternoon at the spring home of the Cleveland Indians. It was "Senior Discount" day at Chain of Lakes Park, and all the lucky senior citizens from Ohio were there to take in the game between the Indians and the Cincinnati Reds. With my lack of hair, including a few gray ones already, I fit right in with the older crowd. With my love for baseball history, I rejoiced with the old-timers, too, when Bob Feller, showed up to play "catch" with some lucky kid before the game.

Bob Feller is in his eighties now, but he still throws better than I do. I did my best to catch him on my camcorder until I heard word that he would be signing autographs in the food court behind the bleachers. I am no longer an autograph hound, but Bob Feller changes things. I made my way down to the food court where a line had already formed in the warm Florida sun. The line led up to a little umbrella-covered table where one of baseball's heroes passes his March afternoons.

Bob Feller joined the Cleveland Indians at age sixteen back in 1936. A scout signed the farm boy from Iowa for one dollar and an autographed baseball. He went to the majors immediately, and struck out fifteen St. Louis Browns in his first start. Soon afterwards, he set an American League record by striking out seventeen in a single game. He then went home to finish high school.

A couple of years later, "Rapid Robert" pitched the only opening day no-hitter in baseball history, the first in a long list of incredible feats. That list includes the fastest pitch ever clocked (104 miles per hour), a pitch that outran a speeding motorcycle.

Feller's career was legendary, but his wartime service smack dab in the middle of that great career garnered attention, too. He joined the Navy the day after Pearl Harbor was attacked, in spite of being classified as a farmer and the sole supporter of his widowed mother. He fought in the Pacific aboard the U.S.S. Alabama and received six battle citations. To keep in shape for his return to baseball, he would jog laps around the battleship between Japanese air attacks.

When World War II ended, Feller returned to baseball and promptly pitched his second no-hitter, this time against the Yankees, striking out Dimaggio and crew en route to a twenty-six-win season. Feller retired in 1956, and he was inducted in the Baseball Hall of Fame in 1962.

And I met him. By my turn, Mr. Feller was trying to eat a hot dog with mustard in between autographs. When I sat down across from him under the umbrella, I actually felt butterflies in my stomach. I don't know why, but I was as nervous as if I was staring down a Randy Johnson fastball—or Feller's. He signed his name, posed for a picture, and I headed back to watch the game. Nothing too special, I guess. But it was special to me.

You see my dad was a good baseball player. My dad was a pitcher. My dad was born the same year Bob Feller was born, and my dad fought on battleships in the Pacific in World War II. My dad spoke highly of Feller's talent somewhere along the way in our countless games of catch in the backyard. And Bob Feller's arms—I've seen those arms up close, long before I ever saw the Hall of Fame pitcher.

My dad is gone now, but at that Spring Training game I connected with him again as I watched a legend play catch with a kid in that warm Florida sun. I wished it were a different little boy, and a different old man. Instead, I ended up with an autograph and a picture; those will have to do.

But unexpectedly, I encountered my very first hero again. And I smiled.

I love Spring Training.

Father
May our hearts always keep our most special
memories stored away in a special place.
Amen

A: The Chicago Cubs (In sixteen games in 2004, the Cubbies drew 189,692 fans.)

Week 2: Golf Miracles

trivia

Q: What is the lowest score for a round in the Masters?

"Hope means expectancy when things are otherwise hopeless."—G. K. Chesterton

The clouds rolled back, the sky opened, and a voice from the heavens proclaimed, "A miracle has occurred. Al broke one-hundred in a round of golf."

If you missed the television coverage, it really happened. ESPN has declared it an "instant classic." Rush Limbaugh is convinced it has something to do with my being white. I ignore the pundits. Next to my wedding day, the birth of my children, my baptism, and … well, a lot of other days, it was the best day of my life.

I had not played over ten rounds of golf in my life—and none of those within months of each other—so the accomplishment qualifies as borderline miraculous. It's like Phil Mickelson winning a major (wait, he did that already). That's okay. I did it, too! Stop the presses. Miracles have not ceased.

The weather was simply gorgeous, mid-seventies, blue skies, puffy white clouds, and a breeze. The course was not even close to being crowded, and my friend Tandy, along with some helpful advice, let me use his awesome driver all afternoon. Plus, I played free. I'm telling you, someone was smiling on me.

The front nine was typical me, with lots of double-and triple-bogeys. My scorecard had a fifty-six on it halfway through the course, which I'm sad to say, wasn't that bad for the way I play golf.

And then, something happened. The spirit of Tiger Woods (or maybe Tony the Tiger) came over me, and I played, "Grrr-eat!!!" I actually shot par on number ten. At that point, my day would have been complete, but unbelievably, I had another par on number eleven. On number twelve, I missed a putt for par by an inch, and then tapped it in for a bogey. On thirteen, a long par five, I actually shot a long par five! This was crazy!

On the next four holes, a bit of sanity returned, but my putting still kept the good times coming with three bogeys and a double-bogey. As we approached eighteen, nervous and excited, I totaled up my score so far—a ninety-four heading into the par four final hole. Suddenly, I was really nervous. Instead of confidence, my doubting self mentioned that I might not ever have the chance in this lifetime to break a hundred again, so I'd better do it now.

I teed off on eighteen with Mr. Tandy's great big driver and hit a crappy slice to the right, but still playable. My second shot was only semi-crappy, off to the right of the green next to the cart path. My arms were numb on the third shot, an attempt to use my nine-iron. I topped it, dribbling my golf ball awkwardly up on the green within ten feet of the cup. My trusty putter finished it off with a par and a ninety-eight for the round!

I declined all interviews. I was too emotional.

Sometimes, it seems, everything just comes together right. Oh, I know it doesn't happen often; at least it doesn't for me, but every once in a while everything seems to fall into place. That's what happened that day to me on a golf course.

I immediately looked forward to my next round of golf. I had a strong suspicion that it would be much worse, but that didn't deter my desire in the least. It might not be worse. There was at least a chance that it would be just as good, or even better. Hope is a wonderful thing.

Your life might not look so hopeful right now. Lord, help you, it might look as bad as the way I play golf. Yet I'll tell you, if I can break a hundred one gorgeous afternoon, a Creator big on mercy can offer you hope as well.

After that, I can guarantee that your whole outlook on the game will be different.

Father,
Our only hope is You. From early in the morning 'til late at night, our only hope is You.
Through Jesus,
Amen

A: 63 (Nick Price in 1986; Greg Norman in 1996)

Week 3: March Madness 

trivia

Q: Who won the first Final Four?

"Nobody roots for Goliath."—Wilt Chamberlain

Welcome to our morning pop quiz. Vocabulary words. Multiple choice.

#1: The Big Dance
(a) The senior prom
(b) The NCAA Basketball Tournament
(c) Janet Jackson and Justin Timberlake at the Super Bowl

#2: Cinderella
(a) A famous fairy tale
(b) A team that wins unexpectedly in the NCAA Basketball Tournament
(c) The best heavy metal group of all time.

#3: Sleeper
(a) A type of sofa that is useful for company
(b) An unheralded team that might win the NCAA Basketball Tournament
(c) Rip Van Winkle

#4: March Madness
(a) Spring fever
(b) The NCAA Basketball Tournament
(c) An unusual malady associated with green beer consumption on St. Patrick's Day.

#5: Diaper Dandy

(a) An absorbent, non-leaking diaper

(b) A very good freshman basketball player

(c) The story of the messiest diaper a person has ever seen.

#6: Bracketology

(a) A nonsense word that doesn't deserve usage in the English language

(b) The study of the NCAA Basketball Tournament, including suggestions on how to predict the outcome (such as always picking at least one 12 seed to upset a 5 seed)

(c) A science class I wasn't smart enough to take in high school.

#7: Office Pool

(a) Sick days that co-workers donate to one another out of compassion;

(b) A contest on company time to see who can predict the winners in the NCAA Basketball Tournament

(c) The collection of drool found on my desk from sleeping on the job.

Okay, turn in your papers.

For those of you that answered mostly "a" on the quiz, you are a fairly normal human being. For those answering "b," you are a sports fan. For those who responded mostly with "c," might I suggest professional therapy?

Sports fans might want to keep the quiz for tutoring purposes. Or not. Who knows, when your co-workers notice you fretting laboriously over a document, they might not know it's your tournament bracket. They may actually think you're working.

I am not sure why we sports fans love this time of year more than any other. Maybe it has something to do with baseball players warming up in Florida, but I suspect it is mostly the dramatic dreams of teenage hoopsters splashed all over television that weekend, the greatest sports weekend of them all.

Some little team will pull off a miracle. Some unknown player will hit a last second shot and unleash joyful pandemonium on a college campus. It is the drama of sports on its highest level, and we sports lovers devour it every year.

And I think it's because we still dream about it, too.

There's something about the underdog coming out on top. And if the sports fans will allow me the apparent sacrilege, I believe the Cinderella story goes deeper than the Big Dance (or even fairy tales or heavy metal bands for the rest of the world). I think it is the spiritual story of mankind.

It is Noah working on his boat. It is Joseph in an Egyptian prison. It is David marching toward Goliath. It is Elijah on Mount Carmel. It is Daniel in the dark with lions. And it is God becoming a baby, cradled in the arms of a teenage girl.

It is the Beatitudes Jesus taught us. The Great Reversal. The Kingdom of God.

And we still dream about it. We cannot help it; it is hard-wired into humanity.

The funny thing is that Jesus said that it is more than just a dream.

Father,
May our inner longings for upsets be realized.
Through Jesus,
Amen

A: The Oregon Ducks in 1939

Week 4: Opening Day

trivia

Q: Who has the major league record for the most Opening Day home runs?

"Baseball is like church. Many attend, but few understand."—Wes Westrum

In the spring of 2003, even though our nation was at war, baseball season opened as scheduled. Festive, opening day activities found large crowds back in their familiar seats at the ballpark, cracking open peanuts and singing a hearty, "Take Me Out to the Ballgame."

Both Cubs' fans and Red Sox fans renewed their annual battle cries: Maybe this will be the year. Fans of every team tuned in or traveled in person to kick off a new season, in hopes that their team would emerge next fall as World Series champions.

One of my friends at church is about the biggest baseball fan I know. He is a diehard Braves fan, and he never misses Opening Day. He was somewhere in the stands that Monday at Turner Field, as dependable as the calendar. But I, on the other hand, am a Cardinals fan. Lucky for me, ESPN2 carried "our" opening day game against Milwaukee. I rode the emotional roller coaster on my sofa, sighing in agony, and erupting in applause in the topsy-turvy game that ended with my team winning, 11-9.

Baseball has long been called "America's Pastime," and I think that's appropriate. When the winter subsides and the grass appears, the athletes with the caps and gloves and funny-looking pants emerge stretching, swinging, hitting, and playing catch in the new sun. Six months later, when we all go inside to endure the winter, these harbingers of spring disappear, too. They will be back, though. Baseball fans count the days.

In fact, baseball often appears larger than life. Its heroes—Ruth, Mays, and Mantle—are American icons. Jackie Robinson was the focal point for American desegregation. Lou Gehrig's disease—well, it was named "Lou Gehrig's Disease." And when World War II erupted, the best players in the game like Bob Feller and Ted Williams signed up and fought alongside the rest of us. Yes, baseball is pure America.

Things have changed, though. Performance-enhancing drugs are suspected. The salaries are downright ridiculous. Going to a game requires a small bank loan. No current players are in line to fight our wars. The kids are even different. Instead of lazy afternoons playing catch with their dads, or pick-up games of "stickball" in the street, most kids spend quality baseball time in front of a television playing video games.

No, it is not the same anymore.

Still, I love Opening Day. The exact reasons why elude me, but I think it has something to do with a reminder of something better. Even on television, when I saw the green grass in St. Louis and the lazy fans eating hot dogs in the sun; when I saw a perfect bunt hit to put the Cardinals ahead and heard the crowd roar its applause; when I saw perfect strangers full of smiles giving each other "high-fives" in the stands—yes, it reminded me that there is something good hiding below the surface of humanity.

Baseball may have been much better in the past, but I excuse myself to cherish those memories—not to mourn for them, but to hold on to the remnants of something better. And to dream. To dream of the beauty behind a game America calls its own.

That may be why I cling to the religious end of following Jesus, too. Sure, there's more problems there than I care to think about, but even Sundays—when I allow them—can take me back to a day when things were better, when discipleship was less cluttered and more pure, and when everything made more sense.

You'll find me in the stands there too this weekend. Sharing the day with friends, with family, and with strangers—a group of people all rooting for the same team. We will experience together the ups and downs of our season, but in the end we all seem to know, our hopes and dreams will reach October, and a championship for the ages.

Enjoy both seasons.

Father,
May we discover our spot on Your team, and may
we hold on to the true significance of every season.
In the name of Jesus,
Amen

A: Frank Robinson (8)

Week 5: The Distance Runner 

trivia

Q: What is the distance running endurance record for a female over twenty-four hours?

"We often find that we were better persons just after our conversion than we are after many years of being a Christian. Every day that passes should make us more like Christ, but we tend to grow cooler rather than warmer."—Thomas à Kempis

I once was a teenage distance runner for three reasons: First, I loved sports almost more than life. Second, I attended a small school where track and field was the only spring sport. Third, I was too weak for the strength events, too slow for the sprints, and I couldn't jump. That left my personal specialty, running slow for a long time. I wasn't world class, but at our level, I was pretty good.

This may sound strange, but I think a large part of any success I had was mental. No, I didn't make it up. I mean that I was good at the mind games, and running distance races definitely involves the mind. More than simply convincing your body to go when it cries stop, and even more than learning to set a pace, distance races involve strategy. The best part of that is messing with the minds of your competitors. I learned how to disguise my breathing in a tight race to gain a psychological advantage, appearing to not struggle as much as the others. I learned how to eat away at someone's lead and eventually overtake him. And, importantly, I learned how to hold off a challenger from behind.

In another effort to get back in shape, I began making regular appearances at a local track, located conveniently across the street from the hospital emergency room (saves on mileage for the ambulance fleet). Sad cases like me are always there. Elderly folks placed on exercise regiments by their physicians are always there, too. Homeless guys hang out on park benches.

I made it to where I walked a mile and jogged another without stopping at the emergency room. I was doing that very thing one day, feeling quite proud of myself. I strutted past a ninety-five year old lady AND her walker, thank you very much. I glided past an overweight man twice my age. Then, I noticed that the race was on.

Looking back, I noticed a girl maybe twenty years old. She was running and gaining on me. She had on a tight outfit to show off her belly button, and—I hate to say it, but—she ran like a girl. I could not let her pass me. All of my skills came back instantly. I sped up my pace. I peeked over my shoulder (left shoulder, always the left) to keep an eye on my lead. I rounded the corner for the stretch run, and the world held its breath. A homeless man sat up to see the thrilling finish. The elderly couple pointed in breathless anticipation. A carload of young boys stopped to stare (well, I think that was more for the girl than the race). I burst across the finish line, arms thrust high in the air. Music from *Rocky* blasted from somewhere in the distance! I've still got it!!!

Well, whatever I've got, I hope there's a shot for it. What I've got is embarrassingly lowered standards.

Other than confirming my idiocy, this isn't a big deal. Our bodies are made to grow and then begin an inevitable decay. Sure, I know of exceptions, but even they get to the point where the body begins to break down, too. It is an unavoidable part of life.

But it doesn't have to be an unavoidable part of spiritual life. We may laugh at the physical fitness problems that come with age. We can't help them. And yet, I worry that we laugh about spiritual decay that should never happen. The Bible says we begin as babies in Christ, but the rest of our lives are meant to witness growth. There is not a point where we attain spiritual maturity, followed by an inevitable decline. Instead, we are to grow until we reach full maturation in Heaven.

I've heard it said often that "once out of the water," a new Christian is ready to take on Satan. Later, the Christian changes his sights to wanting to save his community. "Maybe I can just save my family" comes along next, followed, of course, by just hoping to make it in myself. We laugh at that, recognizing its familiarity, smirking at the idealism of youth. I just think we probably ought to stop smirking.

I'm a sorry distance runner now. I want to be a better one spiritually.

> *Father,*
> *Protect us, of course, but let us at him.*
> *Amen*

A: 150 miles by Russian, Irina Reutovich (1998)

Week 6: The Final Four

trivia

Q: How many freshmen have been named the Most Outstanding Player of the Final Four?

"Tell me to what you pay attention, and I will tell you who you are."—José Ortega y Gasset

I live one hundred miles from New Orleans, and through what must have been divine intervention, I was a winner in the annual Final Four ticket lottery in 2003. I won the right to sit in the rafters of the Superdome and watch the greatest game of the season when Kansas battled Syracuse for the national championship.

I took my friend Herman with me to the semifinals. We traveled over early in the afternoon, expecting heavy traffic, but finding it not so bad. We expected to park a long ways away, but we found a nice spot close by. We expected to pay a lot for cheap refreshments and souvenirs. We were right about that.

I had a blast. I ran into Gary Williams of Maryland, the coach from the previous year's national champions. I took his picture and shook his hand. I should add that as I shook his hand, I froze like a boy asking a girl on a date. Later, I decided that I should have offered a confident, "Great season, Coach," and a firm handshake. Instead, I acted like a blooming idiot. Oh well, some people just fold under pressure.

Handling pressure is what I thought about that night. Over 54,000 people crowded into the Superdome to watch a basketball game. I was astounded to watch youngsters like Carmelo Anthony calmly put in a wonderful performance in front of that massive crowd, not to mention the millions around the world watching on television.

How can you perform like that under such pressure? That's what I thought about when my nose stopped bleeding and oxygen masks descended from the Superdome roof.

I played basketball. I never played in front of 54,000 people, but I did find myself under pressure. Important free throws with games on the line. Important possessions with the clock running down. And I'll admit, in spite of what some may say, I did think about the people in the stands. I think all athletes do to some extent. We (notice how I include myself with athletes—he, he) all want to impress the crowd, and that creates pressure.

Here's the deal, though. Whether there are 54,000 fans paying big bucks at the Superdome, or fifty-four moms and dads at a Saturday morning JV game, every athlete has the face of one person in his or her mind when performing. One face above all the rest. It may be that girl you hope to impress, or a dad that you cannot please. It may be an older sibling whose standard you hope to live up to, or a potential friend you want to like you. All of us play for one person. That is how Carmelo Anthony could play as he did amid such pressure. He was not playing for me. He couldn't care less about me. He was playing for one person. I don't know whom, but I guarantee it.

At least that's my theory, and I'm sticking to it.

The spiritual application is penetrating. In this great big game of life, you and I play for one person, too. Whether major television networks want to broadcast our spiritual battle or it would bore our own cats, we all play for someone. It may be we are hoping to impress some family member or a friend, a preacher or a neighbor, a parent or a spouse. It could be that we want to impress some theoretical person that does not exist.

It could be that we play with Jesus at the forefront of our minds. That's what the dude that wrote Hebrews told us to do. In theory, that's what we know to do. In reality, we often seek to impress others. At least it is "others" that take the forefront of our minds. I find that sad. For you see, Jesus is the most relaxing fan base of them all. Jesus is pleased with our best, no matter what anyone else thinks. Pleasing Jesus is a burden that can only be defined properly with words like "easy" and "light."

On Championship nights, someone emerges as a hero in the eyes of the sports world. On those same nights, others leave characterized as a failure.

For every one of those players, though, what really matters in the end is the opinion of that one person.

In my mind, I'd like that person to be Jesus.

Father,
As we play the game of life, may we focus our attention on playing only for You. The rest, we know, doesn't really matter.
Through Jesus,
Amen

A: Three (Arnie Ferrin of Utah in 1944; Pervis Ellison of Louisville in 1986; Carmelo Anthony of Syracuse in 2003)

Week 7: Field Of Dreams

trivia

Q: In the movie, *Field of Dreams,* what book is Terence Mann reading when Mark interrupts the ball game with news of foreclosure on the farm?

"You can't do anything about the length of your life, but you can do something about its width and depth."—Evan Esar

Although I'm always on the lookout for significance, it sometimes sneaks past my watch; one night I barely caught it. I had just returned home from a night of tennis with my teenage daughter when I found my wife watching *Field of Dreams.* Now, as a fan of both sports and inspirational movies, this ranks in my book as a very good thing to do.

When we sat down, the movie had reached its climax. Ray (Kevin Costner) was about to lose the farm but had decided that his magical baseball field was worth the risk. The doctor had crossed back over from the field of dreams to save Ray's daughter's life, and the forever young "old-timers" called it a day. They invited Terence Mann (James Earl Jones) to disappear into the mysterious corn stalks with them, and Ray and family resolved to turn in for the night, too. That's when it happened.

The catcher, the last player on the field, was still packing his bags when Ray understood his identity; it was his father. With more emotion than my wife's tear ducts could handle, Ray's father (as a young man) walked across the field to meet his son. They shook hands, discussed the possibility that Iowa might be heaven, and then, just before his dad headed toward the corn stalks, Ray ased, "Dad? Wanna play some catch?" And they did. In a world where dreams come true, a father and son played catch.

Okay, I may sound sappy, but it started to get to me, too.

I spent a lot of time in a back yard playing catch with my dad when I was a kid. Even though he was fifty years older than I was, we spent countless hours together every night with well-worn gloves and worn-out baseballs until we couldn't see anymore. It had been nearly a decade since I drove my dad to the hospital the last time, just days before he died. One of our last conversations involved both of our wishes that we could play catch once more. We knew it would not happen.

So it got to me a little bit. Dreaming of a world where we could play catch again. Imagining what it would be like to suddenly meet my father again, this time as a young man, and throw a baseball around under a burning sunset. Picturing his smile as I introduced him to his granddaughter, who feels as if she has met him already.

I could have pouted if the dream wasn't so wonderful to imagine. I suddenly had the desire to find everything I had that reminded me of my dad and to settle into a daydream world where a baseball field contains the wildest dreams of all.

You see I almost missed the significance. Did you catch it, too?

Just as I was about to spend the rest of my evening sadly wishing for days gone by, I recognized what I had been doing: Playing tennis with my beautiful teenage daughter. We had played at Inner Harbor Park, with seagulls and pelicans traversing the horizon. The sun was setting in all its majesty when we arrived, and the early summer heat on the Coast had been replaced with a nice, cool breeze. The scene could not have been nicer as we had played into the night. No, heaven cannot be in Iowa. That was a movie. Instead, I think it might be in southern Mississippi.

There is a time for all things, according to the Bible. There is a time to move on in life. I still miss playing catch with my dad, but I learned last night that wishing for the past should not replace the memories being made in the present. I don't want to waste the time I have living in the past. It is my time to assume the other side of the game.

I would love to play catch with my dad again, but Jesus summed it up this way: Do to others what you wish would happen to you.

Now that I noticed, that's what I plan to do.

Father,
May we not miss life along the way.
Through Jesus,
Amen

A: *The Baseball Encyclopedia*

Week 8: An Amazing Shot

trivia

Q: What is the record for the oldest person to score a hole-in-one?

"It is hard to fail, but it is worse never to have tried to succeed."—Theodore Roosevelt

It will go down as one of the greatest shots in the history of golf. No, I'm not speaking of Larry Mize's amazing chip-in birdie on number eleven at Augusta in 1987. No, I'm not speaking of Lee Trevino's shot on number seventeen at St. Andrew's in 1972 to steal the British Open from Jack Nicklaus. And no, Tiger Woods was not involved.

The shot did take place at St. Andrew's, though not the famed course in Scotland. It occurred at the St. Andrew's Golf Club a couple of miles from my house. I was the golfer, and my shot will live in infamy in the minds of all five witnesses there that day.

I do not recall which hole we were on. It really doesn't matter because the hole did not come into play at all during this shot. Nor did the fairway. Nor did any water hazard, sand trap, deep rough, unfortunate houses, or passing birds. In fact, the entire historic moment took place on the tee box.

I remember someone else teed off first. I remember my golf cart partner and I watched that shot, and for some reason, both decided to change the club we would each use. I put my new Christmas present driver back in my bag and pulled out my one-iron.

When my turn came, I teed the ball up a bit high (which will matter shortly), and as everyone else watched in breathless anticipation, I swung that trusty one-iron with a mighty swing. As I followed through, my tee sailed ten yards out of the tee box.

The tee turned out to be the only thing that sailed out of the tee box. I looked down to see the golf ball that I had planned on hitting sitting directly below where I had it perched on the now launched tee. I had somehow swung my club head just below the golf ball and hit the tee out from under the ball.

I really think that in my years of playing golf that was by far my most amazing feat. It was nothing short of miraculous.

Of course it did nothing for my golf game and even less for my self-confidence. It seemed to buoy everyone else's, though ("Well, at least I didn't do what Al did!"). I soon learned that out of all the combined golfing experiences of those in our group, no one had ever seen what I accomplished. Some offered that it might not ever be seen again.

I am now a storied part of the vast realm of golf lore, thank you very much. I am so very proud.

Well, what do you do? I tried to laugh with everyone else at myself. I kept hacking away at those golf balls the rest of the afternoon. I finished the course with my customary forty to fifty shots over par. And now, I am telling many people around the world that I do not know of my humiliation.

I'm not sure why I'm doing the last thing, but the rest makes perfect sense. When you fall flat on your face, you just have to get up and keep going, right? If at first you don't succeed, try, try again. If you fall off the horse, you've got to climb back in the saddle. Unless the saddle fell off, too—then you need to do a better job of putting the saddle on. Or unless you broke some bones—then you need to go to the hospital.

But you get the point: When life knocks you down, go down swinging, even if you miss the golf ball entirely.

C. S. Lewis once revealed his estimation of how God sees us in *The Screwtape Letters*. He wrote, "As long as the will to walk is there, he is pleased with their stumbles." In other words, a parent doesn't despise a child for falling when he is learning how to walk. Instead, a parent encourages the child to keep on trying until he gets it.

I guess I'll keep doing that with golf.

I hope we will all keep doing that with life.

Father,
May we all keep our will to walk, and may You always be pleased with our tottering efforts.
Through Jesus,
Amen

A: 99. (In January 1985 Otto Bucher from Switzerland holed-in-one at the age of 99 on La Manga's 130-yard 12th hole.)

Week 9: Obstacles

trivia

Q: How many clay court matches in a row did Chris Evert win?

"Obstacles are those frightful things you see when you take your eyes off the goal."—Hannah More

Although I devote most of my attention to the "big three" sports, I have tinkered around a bit with most of the rest in some fashion. I own a hockey puck (Lord knows why). I've played one brief and ugly season in a community volleyball league. I've become knowledgeable in the sport of disc golf. I've even tried to pole vault.

Out of all these "other" sports, however, one of my favorites to play is tennis.

My oldest sister taught me the sport as she used me for practice for a college class she had to take. I enjoyed it right away. In fact, I spent more afternoons than I can remember playing tennis up against the massive brick wall of the church building directly across the street from our house. I never could beat that stinking brick wall.

It turns out that tennis can be pretty entertaining to watch, too.

By the time I started watching the sport, the male version featured a trio of heroes in Bjorn Borg, Jimmy Connors, and John McEnroe. I, for some reason, always pulled for Ivan Lendl instead. He had cool wristbands.

Hey, I was a stupid kid!

On the female side of the net, there were only two options to consider: Chris Evert-Lloyd, and Martina Navratilova. They seemed to face each other in the finals of every tournament. I'm not wanting to sound sexist or anything, but I think I always pulled for Chris Evert because I thought she was pretty.

Give me a break. I was an adolescent boy!

She was a dang good tennis player, too.

Chris Evert was one of the world's finest tennis players with our without the "-Lloyd" attached to the end of her name. She had tremendous powers of concentration, and like most top tennis players, never lost her focus.

Once during a junior tournament, someone left a chair near the back line. Whenever Chris went back for a shot, she continually bumped into that chair. But she never moved it. After the match, someone asked her why she hadn't moved the chair that kept getting in her way. Chris looked puzzled.

"What chair?" she asked.

I love that story.

We are often very successful at least at one thing: finding excuses for why we can't accomplish our goals. In Chris Evert's case, we would not only find the chair at fault, but also blame the sun, the court, our racket, breakfast, and poor parenting. We could come up with quite a list.

What I'm wondering is what we could accomplish if we were totally absorbed in our goals, not our obstacles.

Now, this thought could mean different things to many different people. Some might decide to bury themselves in goals for financial or occupational success. Others might dedicate their focus to family. Maybe others even in church work. I don't advise any of the above (including church work).

Instead, I suggest that our single-mindedness be in knowing God. I think everything else will, in His way, take care of itself.

Father,
May we seek You with all of our being.
Through Jesus,
Amen

A: 125

Week 10: The Splendid Splinter

trivia

Q: What uniform number did Ted Williams wear?

"The difference between the impossible and the possible lies in a man's determination."—Tommy Lasorda

Unfortunately, most of the world will remember Ted Williams in frozen form. To baseball fans, however, he will be remembered for amazing hitting and stubbornness.

The statistics are overwhelming. The man known as "The Splendid Splinter" won baseball's Triple Crown twice, hit 521 home runs, had a lifetime batting average of .344, played in eighteen All-Star games, and was named American League MVP two times. He is also the last player to hit .400 in the major leagues, hitting .406 in 1941.

That 1941 performance revealed something of the character of Ted Williams, too. No major league player had hit .400 since 1923, and going into the season's last day, Williams' was hitting .3995 (which would be rounded up to .400). Manager Joe Cronin offered to sit his star out of the season-ending doubleheader scheduled that day to assure Williams the honor. After struggling with the decision, Williams decided that he should play and earn the record. Did he ever. Six hits in eight at-bats and a .406 season.

Williams was such an amazing left-handed pull hitter that he had a defensive maneuver named after him. The famed, "Williams shift," employed by opposing teams, shifted most fielders to the right side of the diamond to try to stop his famed line drives. In 1946, though, he clinched a pennant for the Red Sox by hitting an inside-the-park home run to an empty left field. As the stats confess, "The Shift" didn't slow him down. Baseball fans also wonder how much he would have accomplished if he hadn't sat out five seasons for military service and injuries.

Did I mention that Ted Williams was also stubborn?

In 1940, after his parents divorced, Williams lived with his eventual wife in Boston. The Beantown's conservative media gave him a hard time for this as well as his slow start at the plate. Williams developed a grudge. When his performance picked up, he refused to tip his hat to the Boston fans. Of course, the heckling and intimidation from the media increased, and by season's end, Williams made it clear that he wanted out of Boston. His teammates rallied around him, preventing that move, but his grudge did not move. He refused to tip his hat to Boston fans for the remainder of his career. Only in 1991, at a fiftieth anniversary celebration of his historic season, did he borrow a Red Sox hat (since he didn't own one) to tip it to the fans.

Stubbornness is hard to portray as a positive quality, but it was this hardheaded determination that allowed Williams to arguably accomplish his lifelong goal of becoming the greatest hitter that ever lived. To Williams, hitting was his craft, and he studied and worked at it harder than anyone. He worked at perfecting his swing every day, regardless of where he had to do it. Eventually, he determined that his feet needed to be twenty-seven inches apart for his stance. He refused to let his bats touch the ground (they might pick up moisture), and he would make sure that each bat weighed a perfect thirty-three ounces. In 1971, he wrote a book called "The Science of Hitting," which many baseball coaches today consider the bible of hitting fundamentals.

When I think of this stubbornness, combined with Williams's amazing lifetime accomplishments, I wonder if followers of Jesus need a healthy dose of it, too. We may wonder from time to time why we accomplish so little. We may attribute it to the fact that the world is self-centered, but the reality may lie in the mirror.

Maybe what it will take to change the world is a few individuals who dedicate their lives to one thing—living life in such a way that someone might say, "There goes the greatest example of Jesus that ever lived." Not for personal glory, mind you, but for His. That decision may lead us to put everything on the line in a season-ending doubleheader. It may require hard work every single day. The goal is worth it, though, don't you think?

Who would have thought that a hardheaded baseball legend like Ted Williams has a lesson for Christians? Well, he does. Now, who's stubborn enough to accept it?

Father,
May we make a lifetime commitment to modeling Jesus, and may we have the determination to do whatever it takes to accomplish that goal.
In His Name,
Amen

A: 9

Week 11: Extreme Sports

trivia

Q: What was the occupation of Edmund Hillary (the original Mt. Everest conqueror)?

"When I enter into my pain rather than run from it, I will find at the center of my pain an amazing insight."—John Powell

Do you remember Aron Ralston?

Well, you might remember him if you picked up his autobiographical book, *Between a Rock and a Hard Place*. Other than that, you may not recognize him by name. Aron is from Aspen, a former mechanical engineer for Intel, and a Carnegie Mellon honors grad. Ring any bells? If not, I suspect you will remember his story. He made headlines through his passion: Aron Ralston is an adventurer.

Being an adventurer is not necessarily newsworthy. Although Ralston has climbed forty-five mountains over fourteen thousand feet tall by himself, most of them in the winter night without oxygen supplies or communication devices, it was in southeastern Utah's Bluejohn Canyon that he unfortunately found his claim to fame.

Covering his press conference in Colorado, *Sports Illustrated*'s Rick Reilly passed on Ralston's rendition of the facts.

The solo adventurer had lowered himself off an eight-hundred-pound boulder when the boulder shifted and pinned his right arm, leaving him unable to escape. Ralston, as expected, tried anything and everything to get the boulder to move: throwing his weight at it, chipping away at the huge rock, all to no avail.

On day three of being trapped, fresh out of ideas, he looked at the knife on his cheap, multiuse tool, and made the only decision he knew to make. He had to cut his own arm. Using a pair of shorts for a tourniquet, he took the knife and did his best to saw into his flesh. Unfortunately, the blade was too dull. Ralston said it "wouldn't even cut my arm hairs," according to Reilly.

But there were no other options. So, for two more days, Aron Ralston worked at cutting off his own right arm with a dull pocketknife.

Eventually, however, he discovered that his plan would not work. In two days, he had successfully sawed through skin and muscle, but he came up against a problem. He needed a bone saw. That's when the crazy thought popped into his head.

"It occurred to me that if I could break my bones up at the wrist, where they were trapped, I could be freed."

I'll spare you the rest of the gory details. Let's just say that Aron Ralston did it. He severed his own right arm, and set himself free.

Of course, the show wasn't over just yet. Without sustenance for five days in the mountains and a freshly amputated right arm, he had to crawl out of Bluejohn Canyon, rappel sixty feet down a cliff, and hike six miles until he made an unforgettable first impression on a couple of foreign hikers.

That, my friends, was a tough week.

Why am I telling you this disturbing story? I've got to tell you a quote from Aron Ralston, reported in Reilly's article for *SI*. When asked how he survived, Ralston stated, "All the desires, joys and euphorias of a future life came rushing into me. Maybe that is how I handled the pain. I was so happy to be taking action."

The book of Hebrews tells us that Jesus did it the very same way. "Fix your eyes on Jesus, who for the joy set before Him, endured the Cross, looked past the shame, and made it back home to be with God." (MSG)

It works the same way for us, too.

For Aron Ralston, it was the thought of drinking margaritas. For Jesus, it was returning to His home in Heaven. For us, it must be something. We will face too much pain along the way to survive without something greater to reach for on the other side.

I'm just thinking this: If a man can do what Aron Ralston did to taste a margarita, what can we overcome with our eyes fixed on the eternal joy in which we believe?

You're right. The sky's the limit.

Father,
May we become adventurers, too, with our eyes
fixed on the joy You offer.
Through Jesus,
Amen

A: Beekeeper

Week 12: The N.B.A. Finals 

trivia

Q: What tragedy occurred to Steve Kerr just before beginning his college career at the University of Arizona?

With doubt and dismay you are smitten,
You think there's no chance for you, son?
Why the best books haven't been written,
The best race hasn't been run.
—Berton Braley

Although I dreamed as a child that I would be a well-respected NBA veteran by this time of my life, professional basketball has got along just fine without me. In fact, the NBA Finals began in 2003 without my watching at all. I had been a semi-San Antonio Spurs fan for quite some time simply because of David Robinson, but after the Western Conference Finals that season, I had another reason: Steve Kerr.

Steve Kerr was a player who personified what I used to tell my basketball teams, "We might be short, but we're slow!" He had a fun career, playing the role of three-point sharpshooter when Michael Jordan was triple-teamed during the championship years. He seemed to have experienced everything a little guy would want in a basketball career. That's why I found it strange that pre-season to see him in uniform when I caught the Spurs in a preseason game in Biloxi. As expected, he sat on the bench most of the game. Seeing it in person, I noticed that Kerr seemed to be a bench favorite, keeping the reserves rolling in laughter for most of the game in spite of his lack of playing time.

But in those Western Finals, for the first time in a long time, I got excited watching a game. It was all about Steve Kerr.

The Spurs needed to win one more game against the Dallas Mavericks to advance to the NBA Finals, and it wasn't looking like it would be that night. The Mavs carried a comfortable, double-digit lead into the fourth quarter. Tony Parker, the Spurs' phenomenal teenage point guard had the stomach flu, and could only play sparingly. Speedy Claxton, the backup point guard, played lots of minutes and played well. In the fourth quarter, Speedy needed a break, so Coach "Pop" sent in Steve Kerr.

You would have thought he had sent in Superman.

Kerr soon hit an open three-pointer to cut into the lead, much to the delight of the bench. He soon hit another three-pointer, and the bench exploded. Shot number three was nothing but net as the Spurs took the lead. He couldn't do it again, could he? Of course! A fourth straight trey left the Spurs bench so excited that David Robinson, the classy seven-footer, was jumping up and down like a three-year-old. Steve Kerr was a hero.

I watched the post-game press conference and became a Steve Kerr fan.

He exuded humility like I had never witnessed in a professional athlete. He admitted openly that there were reasons he didn't play very much—reasons he very much understood. He admitted that he lived a charmed life, that he didn't deserve to play in the NBA at all, and that he wondered every day why he had been so blessed. Above the humility, though, he said something profound: He explained why he still played. He had been asked how that night ranked in his career highlights, and he placed it at the top. He said that this is why he still played; playing for the dream of a night like this. Steve Kerr laces up his high-tops each game to sit on the end of the bench, dreaming that each night just might be the night that he comes in and performs magic. He plays for that dream.

I wonder what we are playing the game of life for? What is it that you dream about? Is it the dream of affecting one more life? Is it the dream of serving one more person in need? Is it the dream of helping one more person find a friend?

I'm a Steve Kerr fan. Sitting on the bench, having a ball, dreaming of one more big night. The opportunity came, and he came through.

I want to live my life like that. Having the time of my life, and dreaming of coming through in the clutch in the only game that matters. I want to taste that kind of success, too. What about you?

Father,
Put us in the game when You need us. We'll be
sitting there in the meanwhile, enjoying the ride,
and dreaming of the chance.
Through Jesus,
Amen

A: Islamic militants in Lebanon murdered his father.

Week 13: Stealing Bases

trivia

Q: What uniform number did Ty Cobb wear?

"Faint not. Fight on. Tomorrow comes the song."
—Maltbie Davenport Babcock

Most people, even non-baseball fans, have heard of Ty Cobb. The grossly misnamed, "Georgia Peach," was one of the greatest baseball players of all time as well as one of the meanest, but no one could dispute his status as a legend. He was one of the first five players elected to the Baseball Hall of Fame, and anything later would have been an insult.

But he was a mean, mouthy little cuss. He once commented that, "When I began playing the game, baseball was about as gentlemanly as a kick in the crotch." Cobb never did much to improve his etiquette. In fact, his famed high spikes seemed intent on making his comment descriptive of his actual style of play.

My favorite Ty Cobb story came late in his life. A nervous writer talked to him about the changes that had taken place in baseball. With the way the game had changed, he asked Cobb how he thought he would fare against today's crop of pitchers. Cobb responded that he would probably hit around .290 or .300.

When asked why the significant decrease in his batting average, whether it was the increased strength of pitchers or maybe the greater variety of pitches today, he stated, "You've got to remember—I'm seventy-three."

He was serious.

Cobb once said, "Baseball is a red-blooded sport for red-blooded men. It's no pink tea, and mollycoddles had better stay out. It's a struggle for supremacy, a survival of the fittest."

And that's the way he played the game.

In addition to his most popular lifetime stats, a .367 batting average and over four thousand hits, Ty Cobb was the most prolific base stealer of his time. In 1915, he set the major league record for stolen bases in a single season by swiping ninety-six. In 1922, Max Carey (Remember him? Neither do I.) moved into second place by stealing a grand total of fifty-one.

Cobb was twice as good, right? Depends on how you look at it.

Max Carey stole his fifty-one bases in just fifty-three attempts, an unbelievable success rate of ninety-six percent. When Ty Cobb set his record with ninety-six steals, he was caught stealing fifty-eight times—more times than Carey even attempted!

Some people could claim that Max Carey was by far the best base stealer baseball had ever seen, but the truth is that no one even remembers him. Ty Cobb goes down as the legend because he was willing to take more chances—and fail more often—so that he could experience more successes.

Paul told the Romans, "Never be lacking in zeal, but keep your spiritual fervor, serving the Lord." (12:11)

I think Paul was saying that we should keep trying to steal some bases. We may fail repeatedly. In fact, we may appear to be a failure many, many times. And yet, those repeated attempts lead us to succeed more than anyone else. We will make a bigger difference in the world because we keep on going for it, time after time after time.

You know the cliché, "If at first you don't succeed, try, try again." Worked for Ty Cobb. I think it's worth a shot for you and I, too.

Father,
In spite of failures, may our dreams of successes
keep us racing toward our goals.
Give us the sign.
Through Jesus,
Amen

A: He did not have a uniform number. (Most teams didn't use numbers until the late-1920s.)

SUMMER

Everyone loves summer.

In fact, there's nothing better in the entire world than a hot summer day in Boston with a Fenway Frank in one hand and a bag of peanuts in the other, screaming through two straight games at the much-hated Yanks.

Well, except maybe standing on Waveland Avenue, glove in hand, acting like a kid again, arguing Pujols versus Sosa while waiting for a big fly. Everyone out there is sweating like pigs, but both sides stop and sing the same song when time pauses in the middle of the seventh inning.

I suppose the best thing in the world could be found in Omaha, Nebraska, hanging out with the college kids at Rosenblatt Stadium for a week or so. I guess it's possible. It sure looks like it on ESPN every year.

But maybe the best time of all is found off a baseball field, out on a boat on a steamy summer morning. Watching the day lazily arrive, fishing pole in hand, wondering if they'll be biting today. It doesn't really matter if they will be or not. The stories aren't affected the least bit by the truth, and besides, life couldn't be any better regardless of what the fish decide to do.

Except possibly on a golf course. After watching the duffers battle Scotland's weather in the British Open, you could swear there's a breeze to blame for those errant tee shots on your summer course, too. But the sun is bright, the clouds are puffy and gentle, the skies are a light, brilliant shade of blue, and the world is respectfully quiet. Until, that is, those sporadic dignified whacks gently remind you that life is good.

Of course, Wimbledon just might be life at it's finest—or at least it's cultured finest. The All England Lawn Tennis Club hosts it's championships every summer, and a seat at center court watching the gentlemen and ladies compete to hoist a gaudy plate above their heads is hard to come by. If you do, you suddenly feel like royalty. You simply have to order the strawberries and cream, along with a spot of tea.

Standing in Paris on the Champs-Elysées watching a bicycle race wouldn't be so bad either. Craning your neck on the crowded sidelines searching for a glimpse of a yellow jerseyed rider, you find yourself screaming for some reason with a French accent. You don't know why. You wonder if you are somewhere close to Heaven.

Some events are so wonderful that even summer cannot contain them every year. The biggest event in the world for a single sport can only be handled every four years, when possibly billions of people wait to hear the news from the aptly named World Cup. It is "football" to the biggest part of the world, and it is an important matter of national pride.

As are the Olympics. Cities compete fanatically for the right to serve as stage to the world, and the winners work tirelessly for years to host the biggest sporting event of them all. It, of course, must be held in the summer. The greatest athletes of every nation show up to assume the stage, dreaming of having a golden medal draped over their neck and singing along as the world observes their particular nation's anthem. And for a few brief moments, at the opening and closing of the games, we believe that sport can somehow bring peace to the world after all.

All in summer.

But I mislead.

In fact, the best things in the world are not in major league ballparks or fishing boats. Not even in Scotland or jolly old England or the streets of Paris. And not even on the stage of the world with a flag being raised and a precious metal draped across your body. Instead, all of these moments combine to inspire the best things in the world; namely, millions of children spread around the globe running and leaping and throwing and hitting and casting and swinging and riding and lifting. All of the children on summer vacation, out in fields, alive and active, and full of dreams.

Yes, everyone loves the summer.

When life is exciting.

Week 14: Fishing Trips 

trivia

Q: How much did the Mississippi state record American eel weigh?

"All our Lord succeeded in doing during his life on earth was to gather together a group of fishermen — the whole church of God and the enterprise of our Lord on earth in a fishing boat!"—Oswald Chambers

Until recently, my lifelong history with fishing consisted of one brief afternoon. I was probably six years old, and my dad thought it mandatory to take his son fishing. What I remember, lo these many years later, are two brief video clips of life that day.

First, I remember sitting by my dad on the bank of Reynolds Lake. He performed the sickening task of shish-k-bobbing a worm on my hook then showing me how to cast the line out into the lake. Then, we sat and watched. Thirty years of my life passed in my mind, though it must have been about thirty seconds, before I heard voices from behind. I turned to look, and the playground equipment at the park was actually calling my name. "Al, please come slide down the slide.... " "Al, please come climb on the monkey bars .... " Well, what's a guy to do? I mean it isn't polite to ignore voices like that. I asked my dad's permission. Frustrated, he understood and told me to go play.

The second memory came from the playground. The voice came from the lake this time, and I recognized it as my dad's asking me to come see something. I ran to his side to see the fish he had caught, a whopper about four inches long. In the brutal honesty of a six-year-old, I responded, "Yeah, can I go back and play?" Frustrated, he agreed.

That, my friends, was my history with fishing.

Everything changed, though, when Shawn took me fishing. Along with his brother, he invited our youth minister and I out for a morning of lessons on the boat. After assuring him that I was functionally illiterate when it came to the sport, he said he wanted me to come anyway. He would take care of everything.

We met at the small craft harbor in Biloxi, and Shawn had everything ready. We boarded the boat, and took off through the cool breeze for my first real fishing trip. We first went to an oyster reef where around twenty boats were already hard at it. Shawn rigged up one of his fishing poles for me, left me alone for a frightening few minutes while I tried to bait my hooks with shrimp, then taught me how to cast.

I was a natural. I caught an eel.

Well, I thought it was a snake at first, and if Shawn wasn't there (and if it wasn't his pole), I believe I would have donated the pole to marine biology. Instead, he grabbed the eel, wrested the hook from his mouth, and let me get back to fishing.

We gave up on two oyster reefs before it became clear that this was just not going to be a red-letter day for fishing. In about three hours, Shawn's brother caught two fish worth keeping. The rest of us fed the undersea world a shrimp buffet.

Finally, we traveled to our third location of the morning, this time behind Deer Island, where we found some success. Overall, we landed seventeen white trout and ground mullet. I caught five, thank you very much. My dad would have been proud.

I honestly couldn't wait to go back. I told Shawn that was what I was most afraid of (well, after drowning, puking, and now eels): just what I need, another hobby.

But it was really fun. It's a whole lot more fun, though, when someone has the boat, the equipment, the bait, and the knowledge. All I had to do was put the bait on the hook, cast my line, and reel 'em in. That's the life.

And that's the life promised us by Jesus.

In effect, in our "fishing for men" expedition, Jesus does for us exactly what Shawn did for me this past Saturday. He gets us in the places we need to be. He gives us the equipment we need for the day. He even manhandles the slimy eels that try to slither into the boat with us. We just put on the bait, cast out our lines, and reel in the catch.

Is this the life or what?

Father,
Thank You for a wonderful voyage, and for providing everything we need. The fish aren't always biting, but we'll keep casting out the line …
Through Jesus,
Amen

A: Five pounds, one ounce (caught in the Mississippi River near Vicksburg by Mitch McLendon of Crystal Springs, Mississippi, on July 12, 1994)

Week 15: Summer Of '79

trivia

Q: Which two-sport athlete made his major league baseball debut in 1979 for the Toronto Blue Jays?

"'This is America,' my father used to say to me, 'and in this country, a smart young fellow like you can grow up and do just about anything.' My dad, no doubt, was thinking doctor, lawyer, teacher, scientist or businessman. I was thinking second baseman, New York Yankees."—Senator Joe Lieberman

I'll never forget that summer. I was still eight years old when my dad and I boarded the bus in the early morning hours. I brought my camera and baseball glove. My dad brought his only son. The bus slowly worked its way northward over the next several hours, making stops at every little town between St. Louis and ours. Eventually, my dad leaned over and whispered, "Look," pointing through the front windshield. I stretched as far as I could and made out the Gateway Arch as a speck in the distance.

We arrived at the city bus station, proclaimed by me "the biggest place in the world," and soon were pedestrians in my first big city. We found a stopping point for the city transit system and waited for one labeled, "Forest Park," to take us to the zoo. We had a great afternoon there, taking pictures, riding the train, getting lost, and paying way too much for snacks. After learning the manly lesson that asking for directions gets you nowhere, we somehow found our way out and boarded the bus to return downtown.

Up close, the Arch looked quite a bit bigger. In fact, when I walked up to its base and slowly raised my head to take in its 630-foot climax, I answered the standing question, "No way." New experiences were fun, but I saw no need in overdoing it.

We finally made it to the ballpark, home of our favorite baseball team. I marveled at the size of the stadium; I stared dreamingly at the sculpture of Stan Musial, and took in all the sights, sounds, and smells that define a trip to the ballpark to me now. We navigated the turnstiles, purchased a forty-cent scorecard, and made our way to our seats in left field. It is almost a cliché, but when the panoramic view of the playing field appeared, it took my breath away. Sure, it was bad Astroturf, and sure I had seen games on television before, but nothing prepared me for the picture.

I'd like to say that the Cards defeated the Cincinnati Reds that night in the ninth with a homerun blast to left field that I snagged over thirty other kids. Not even close. We lost sixteen to four, and the closest I came to catching a ball came when the Reds' back-up catcher, Vic Correll, hit a grand-slam about a hundred feet from me. Nonetheless, the evening was awesome. Sitting behind Lou Brock in his final season, seeing the last part of the Big Red Machine—Bench, Morgan, Seaver, Griffey, and Foster; and being alone with my dad in a sea of fifty-thousand fans combined to make that night one of my best.

When the game ended, we fought our way through the swarm of people, and began our trek back to the bus station. My dad was a cautious man, which leads me to think he hadn't thought this part through. The massive crowd grew smaller and smaller until the only people left on the dark city streets were an impressive collection of winos and homeless people and the two of us. I could sense his uneasiness. His grip on my hand grew tighter, and the pace of our walk grew faster. I just squeezed back and walked faster until we made it back to the station.

Inside the station, my dad bought me a little trophy that says, "I'm a Cardinals Fan." We boarded the bus and rode through the night back to our hometown. I remember nothing of the trip home, except falling asleep on my daddy's lap.

It was a great day, with only one not-so-great memory. I still remember those eyes staring at us on those dark, urban streets, and the feeling that my dad was nervous. That was a new feeling for me. It worried me. But it was a brief worry. Before long, I was asleep in his arms once more.

I've had those same feelings resurface since. There have been times when I've sensed myself spiritually surrounded, and all I wanted was escape. Instead, I've been forced to remember that my calling is not to escape, but to walk. My call is to keep my hand in His, to walk at His pace, and to arrive at the station right beside Him.

I learned that lesson, initially, in the summer of 1979.

Father,
May we hold on tight and keep pace with You.
Thanks for the trip.
Your children

A: Danny Ainge (at age twenty)

Week 16: How You Play The Game 

trivia

Q: How old was Bobby Jones when he retired from competitive golf?

"There is no reward for the loser, but neither should there be for those who don't win honorably. The person who wins unfairly should be set down."
—Knute Rockne

American society is bent on winning and has little regard for losers. Our economy is based on winners. Our entertainment industry, too. In America, winners are rewarded and losers are discarded. That's just the facts, ma'am.

Leo Durocher: "Nice guys finish last."

Knute Rockne: "Show me a good and gracious loser and I'll show you a failure."

George S. Patton: "Americans love a winner. Americans will not tolerate a loser. Americans despise cowards. Americans play to win all the time."

Yet somewhere back in elementary school, I can still hear Mr. Stokes telling us, "It's not whether you win or lose; it's how you play the game."

Yeah, and how you play the game determines whether you win or lose. And I never cared much for losing.

Yet Jesus had a different approach than me and Leo Durocher and Knute Rockne and General Patton. He seemed to agree more with Mr. Stokes. It takes great effort for followers of Jesus Christ to notice, accept, and implement His lifestyle; a lifestyle where all men are really regarded as equals—a life where the losers are loved just as much as the winners.

However, it must be noted that Jesus preached good news, and that good news involved winning instead of losing. Although the Beatitudes are fascinating, one must notice that Jesus did not say that the "losers" of this world should take pride in their status, but that the losers could be proud that they would become the winners. "The first shall be last, and the last shall be first," breathes hope for success, not contentment with seeming failure.

With all this in mind, I pose the question, "Are we playing to win?"

"Winning at all costs" is a negative phrase in most circles although the attitude toward the phrase rests on the definition of the word "winning." What does it mean to truly win?

In the 1925 U.S. Open, hero of the golfing world Bobby Jones penalized himself a stroke for something no one else had seen. When the blade of his club touched the tall grass in the rough, his ball moved slightly. Although this made no difference in the shot, and no one else knew, he added a stroke to his score. That left him in a tie with Willie McFarlane who went on to "win" the playoff.

Fifty-three years later, in the Hall of Fame Classic at Pinehurst, North Carolina, Tom Kite did the exact same thing. His self-imposed penalty resulted in his losing a tournament as well.

When incredulous sports reporters asked both golfers decades apart the same question, a similar answer came forth: There's only one way to play the game.

I do not like to lose. Through my many experiences coming up on that side of the scoreboard, you'd think I would have grown fond of it by now. But I haven't. I really don't like it at all.

But there's only one way to win. Giving your best, playing within the rules, and accepting the outcome is the only way to appreciate it. Anything less cheapens the word.

Just ask Bobby Jones and Tom Kite.

Even Mr. Stokes.

Most importantly, Jesus.

Father,
Thank You for giving us the tools we need to be winners in the greatest game of them all. May we approach the game, knowing the rules, and putting out our greatest effort.
In the Name of Jesus,
Amen

A: Twenty-eight

Week 17: The Minor Leagues

trivia

Q: The Pawtucket Red Sox and Rochester Red Wings played the longest game ever in 1981. How many innings did the game last?

"A continual looking forward to the eternal world is not a form of escapism or wishful thinking, but one of the things a Christian is meant to do. It does not mean that we are to leave the present world as it is. If you read history, you will find that the Christians who did the most for the present world were just those who thought most of the next."—C. S. Lewis

Minor league baseball is a lot of fun if you are looking for something to do.

We traveled over to Mobile, Alabama, with some good friends one evening to take in a game. We sat in the shade with a bit of a breeze to take the edge off the Gulf Coast summer's humidity and watched the Mobile Bay Bears battle the Chattanooga Lookouts.

Early on, we noticed a short, stocky third baseman with the number fourteen and the name Rose on his back take the field for the Reds affiliate out of Chattanooga. It turned out to be Pete Rose, Jr., the spitting image of his famous father.

My friend asked me if I thought his dad was there. I said, "No, but I bet he's got money on it." (Hey, it's a joke!)

One of the great things about minor league action is that not many people show up to watch. As a result, we sat by ourselves on the front row behind third base. Another advantage is that the owners try to drum up attendance by bringing to the park all sorts of entertainment and promotions. We enjoyed a comedian's antics along with some sort of exciting contest with every passing inning.

Also, at least at the Double-A level, the players are pretty impressive. They don't haul in much money themselves; instead, they are young men with a love for a game and a dream. They enjoy giving out baseballs and autographs (my four-year-old got one of each), and they clown around with the entertainment when given a chance. In short, they aren't yet too big for their knickers.

That dream of making it to the "bigs" is inspiring to me. I used to dream about it, too, but a series of unfortunate Little League experiences led me to shelve the dream away. These guys have not shelved their dreams. In fact, they are two steps away from the realization of their dreams. Most of these players will get no closer than where they are now. Some will draw just one step closer. A few will make it. And for that hope, they all keep putting out the effort.

We Christians can relate. In the world we live in now, we too live with a love and a dream—a love for God and a dream of making it to Heaven someday. In many ways, although this world is a far cry from the magnificence and splendor of Heaven, this is a pretty great place. We get to be the players, and we get a taste of what it will be like someday.

The similarities go on.

As with minor league baseball, some of us will make it and some of us will not. A simple reading of Jesus makes this point all too clear. What separates the minor leaguers, however, will be a combination of breaks and talent. Hearts, on the other hand, will separate Christians. Oh, I know we could talk about faith, and I know we could talk about works, but the two are a package deal—and the two are products of the heart.

I cannot tell you where your heart lies. You may know already, or you may be trying to fool yourself. You may have the courage to do as David did and ask God to search your heart for you and show you what He finds.

My prayer for each of us today is this: That our hearts stay set on a dream. That we will not let our embarrassing Little League experiences dissuade us from keeping our heart set on making it to the "show." And that we will all meet there in the clubhouse someday ....

Father,
Search our hearts, and reveal us ...
Through Jesus,
Your dreamers

A: Thirty-three

Week 18: Special Olympics

trivia

Q: The First International Special Olympics Summer Games were held on July 20, 1968, in what stadium?

"How many people stop because so few say, 'Go!'"
—Charles R. Swindoll

I finally did it. I spent six hours at NASA's Stennis Space Center volunteering at the Special Olympics. I had always wanted to do that, but I had never made the time before that Saturday. It was very worthwhile.

I got to be buddies with Bobby Lambert, a thirty-six-year old athlete from Gulfport, Mississippi. Bobby is an interesting guy. He is 6'6 and wears a size-thirteen shoe (had me beat on both counts). Bobby likes two types of music: opera and rap. He is also an accomplished square dancer. He was ready for the Special Olympics to be over so he could go shopping since he needed some new square dancing shoes.

Bobby took second place in the shot put early in the day. He kept getting flack from everyone because he kept his ribbon in his pocket instead of on his shirt. His excuse was that the ribbon would get in his way when he ran the 400-meter run later in the day, and he had big plans for that 400-meter run. When the big moment came, Bobby took second place. He was especially proud because he beat his roommate Robbie. Bobby took his roomie down because he knew how to pace himself.

I've only been once now, but I must say that the Special Olympics are amazing. I found myself wanting to cry, and I wasn't exactly sure why. It really would not have been tears of sadness, but it wouldn't have been tears of joy either. It is hard to find the words, but it wasn't very hard to find the emotions.

My volunteer job was called a "sponsor." As an athlete's sponsor, I had the privilege of marching in to the opening ceremonies right alongside the athletes. Numerous fans lined the sides of the route cheering and waving and smiling the biggest smiles you've ever seen in your life. It was beautiful.

Throughout the day, I saw nothing but encouragers wherever I turned: people running alongside the athletes urging them on, individuals giving hugs to everyone in sight. One young lady was running up to every stranger she could find, showing them her ribbon, followed by a big bear hug free of charge.

I wonder why isn't life more like the Special Olympics? Something is just right about it; something that offers solutions to the wrong all around us. Why don't we listen to Paul's instructions when he told a church in Greece they should "...encourage one another and build each other up?" (1st Thessalonians 5: 11)

If you are like me, I do feel at times like people are lining the parade route and running alongside me in my race. Generally, the feeling seems to be that these people are pointing fingers at me, whispering about me, telling me where I'm wrong. Maybe you feel that way, too. Wouldn't it be nice—just once—to feel like the whole world is on your side and everybody wants to encourage you?

Maybe that's why I wanted to cry. Maybe it had nothing to do with them, but simply with me.

One thing I remembered:

Jesus felt the abuse. If ever a man was not encouraged by those around him and had to walk the runway with others lashing out at him, Jesus did. When you feel that way, remember that Jesus did that just so He could be there for you.

And one more thing:

If you claim to be a follower of Him, remember to be one of those encouragers. That is our job. I give thanks to the great number of people who do that for me in such important ways. I pray that somehow I may be able to do the same for each of them.

Father,
Thank You for teaching us, and thank You for being there for us. Help us to be there for others.
Through Him,
Amen

A: Chicago's Soldier Field

Week 19: Radio Baseball

trivia

Q: Harold Alren of KDKA in Pittsburgh, Pennsylvania, broadcast the first ever baseball game on the radio on August 25 of what year?

"Our expectation of what the human animal can learn, can do, can be, remains remarkably low and timorous."—George B. Leonard

On a thousand mile road trip, I ran across a St. Louis Cardinals baseball game on the radio. The memories came flooding back. I'm not an old-timer by any stretch, but I do at least remember when television stations went no higher than channel thirteen and "having cable" was unknown. As a result, my sports fixation in pre-ESPN days was met sporadically; most often by listening to the Cardinals play baseball on the radio.

KDRS was my home for Cardinal baseball, although they simply transmitted the powerful signal from KMOX out of St. Louis. The voices of Jack Buck and Mike Shannon explained countless tidbits of baseball strategy as I spent hour after hour huddled next to our tiny radio ("Never swing at the first pitch when the pitcher is struggling," a Mike Shannon pet peeve. "Never make the first out of an inning trying to take an extra base"). My young, impressionable mind soaked up every bit of information from these broadcasting legends.

The beauty of listening to baseball on the radio, though, is that it involves the imagination. Listening to the broadcasts required a creative mind. When Kenny Reitz, Tommy Herr, and Keith Hernandez pulled off a 5-4-3 double play, Jack Buck's words and my animated mind painted a picture that had me jumping off the couch in joy. When Ted Simmons or George Hendrick went deep ("It's a long fly ball, deep left field—it might be—it could be ...."), I always captured the thrilling scene in my imagination.

Television changed things. Radio broadcasts still exist, but when it became possible to watch, the radio was pushed to the side. Why listen when you can see?

The Bible tells us that we walk by faith, and not by sight—which may have something to do with listening to baseball on the radio. When I listened, I was filled with anticipation. When the game was close and Mike Shannon said, "Here's the pitch," my heart froze, listening for any sign—a crack of the bat, the roar of the crowd, or the excitement in his next word. Listening filled me with anticipation. I listened for any sign.

Today, in the religious world, there seems to be more looking than listening. We seem to know more than we anticipate. We walk by sight and not by faith. I find that sad.

Read the New Testament. Well, read the whole Bible and you will find the story of a people living in anticipation. Words like "faith" and "hope" permeate the theological aspects of the text because that is what the story describes—a people anticipating something great in the future.

I know we still believe in a Heaven, but I'm afraid we are too occupied with everything we see and know to spend much time on the edge of our seats anticipating God's next move. I don't think we are sitting next to the radio with our hearts frozen, waiting for the next word from the mouth of God much anymore.

When Satan came to tempt Jesus, he first tempted Him to change the rules to meet His selfish physical needs. Jesus responded that man does not live by bread alone, but by every word that comes from the mouth of God. I have preached that in a variety of ways. I'm sad to realize that I've never paid much attention to that last part of Jesus' response.

I guess we've always believed technically that man lives on every word from God. Too bad we think He quit talking two thousand years ago.

God is active in His world today. He is everywhere, effecting the changes He desires. We need to quit walking by sight and only noticing everything He does in retrospect. We need to live in holy anticipation, sitting on the edge of our seats, listening intently for the next clue to what God is doing. We need to live (present tense) on every word that comes from His mouth.

He who has ears, let him hear.

Father,
May our lives be lived on the edges of our seats in
anticipation and with wide-open imaginations of
what You will do next.
In the name of Jesus,
Amen

A: 1921

Week 20 :the Pole Vault 

trivia

Q: Earl Bell, bronze medallist in the 1984 Summer Olympics, set the world outdoor record for the pole vault in what year?

"God answers our prayers. Sometimes the answer is yes. Sometimes the answer is no. Sometimes the answer is, you've got to be kidding!"—Jimmy Carter

Very few things excite me like ambition. Dreamers motivate me. People with vision inspire me. I love to hear the plans of people who want to change the world. I am captivated by inspirational movies. Ambition makes me smile.

I think it makes God smile, too. Why else would Jesus emphasize the fact that all things are possible with God? As Jimmy Carter pointed out, I'm sure God has a variety of responses to our prayers. I think he gets excited with us when our prayers are ambitious.

I tried to pole vault once. My friend, Shawn and I, decided to stay after school one spring and learn how. Our school had a rich vaulting tradition, and though we were distance runners, we thought we'd learn to diversify our talents. Instead, I nearly learned to diversify my body.

I have the body style of an Olympic vaulter, long and lean. Olympic vaulters, however, are strong and fast, too. Plus they can jump. I'm a bit lacking in all three of those very important areas.

We both gave it up before long. We stuck to what we did best.

Several years later, I returned to my own track program as the coach of our successful program. In the same vein of "doing what you do best," I got to tell others what to do. Hey, you know the saying, "Those who can't do, teach," right? Well, I became a coach/teacher, and we kept our pole-vaulting dominance intact.

One day, I took two of my pole-vaulters to buy some poles. We went to one of the best places in the world for that type of shopping. Believe it or not, the hotspot for purchasing poles is Valley View, Arkansas. That, my friends, is the home of Bell Athletics, which is the life's work of Earl Bell.

Earl Bell holds an Olympic medal in the pole vault, is a former world record holder, and a world-class coach for world-class athletes. When we arrived, I tried not to be too obvious that I was in awe of such a great talent, but Earl Bell is not only a great athlete, but also a gracious gentleman.

He began by having my vaulters run-through with a variety of poles to determine the best ones for them. One of my vaulters was fearless. He was fast and strong and would go all out with each jump. Each time he would vault, Earl would laugh out loud. Not at him. It was a laugh of sheer joy. He was delighted to see a young man go all out.

I started thinking; Earl trains guys that vault eighteen or nineteen feet, guys who are headed to the Olympics. My guys might vault eleven feet. Why would he get such pleasure in watching them?

I think it is much more than just his love for the sport. I think it must have been my athlete's lack of fear, his reckless abandon. I think it was his complete trust that this Olympic hero would not give him a pole unless it would support him.

I think God is like that, too. I believe God lets out a laugh of joy when we take Him at his word and go for it. I believe that there is sheer pleasure for God when we ask Him to accomplish great things through us. It is sad that so few of us do.

What are your dreams? Is this just another year of your life, or will you ask God to make history through you this season?

H. Jackson Brown wrote in his best-selling *Life's Little Instruction Book*, "Be bold and courageous. When you look back on your life, you'll regret the things you didn't do more than the ones you did."

Words to remember if you ask me. But if you don't believe me, go spend some time with Earl Bell.

Father,
Bring about Your will on this earth through us.
Change the world. Teach us to dream. Remind us to ask. Increase our faith.
With love,
Your athletes

A: 1976

Week 21: Fifty-Six

trivia

Q: Who performed the song that made famous the phrase, "Where have you gone, Joe Dimaggio?"

"Always do right. This will gratify some people, and astonish the rest."—Mark Twain

When Joe Dimaggio passed away at age eighty-four, I found all the reactions from the sports journalists interesting. It is always interesting, I guess, to see the legacy someone leaves behind. Words like "class" and "hero," and words like "grace" and "dignity" filled the newspaper columns and television airwaves as fans and admirers attempted to describe what the Yankee Clipper had meant to them.

What will always be associated with Joltin' Joe Dimaggio, however, even more than Marilyn Monroe, is "The Streak." For older men who remember, mentioning Marilyn Monroe and "Streak" in the same sentence might cause heart palpitations. Don't let your mind wander. Every sports fan knows what I'm talking about instead.

"The Streak" came in 1941 when Joe Dimaggio hit safely in fifty-six consecutive games. The record has stood for over six decades now, and though a handful of players have flirted distantly with it, many baseball fans wonder if it will ever be broken.

This isn't the first legendary baseball record to seem unbreakable, though:

Lou Brock's 118 stolen bases? Stolen by Rickey Henderson.

Babe Ruth's 714 home runs? Blasted out of the park by Hank Aaron.

Roger Maris's 61 homers in '61? Topped by McGwire, then Sosa, then Bonds ....

Lou Gehrig's 2,130 consecutive games? Outlasted by Cal Ripken, Jr.

Ty Cobb's 4,191 base hits? Slapped by Pete Rose.

What makes Dimaggio's record so "unbreakable" when all of the other unbreakable records have gone down? I think it has to do with "consistent excellence."

Neither Lou Brock nor Rickey Henderson stole a base every day. Neither Babe Ruth nor Henry Aaron, neither Roger Maris, Mark McGwire, Sammy Sosa, nor Barry Bonds hit home runs every day. Sure, Lou Gehrig and Cal Ripken, Jr. played every day, but they had some bad games. And obviously, the hit kings, Ty Cobb and Pete Rose, never matched Dimaggio's streak in their careers.

It is hard to perform "well" every single day. Everyone has his "up" days and "down" days. I believe that's why all of baseball speaks with awe when they speak of "The Streak." Baseball historians will quickly remind you, too, that after Dimaggio's streak ended at fifty-six games, he went on to hit safely in his next sixteen games as well. Seventy-two out of seventy-three games.

Amazing.

How do Christians even attempt to pursue this amazing concept of "consistent excellence?" How do we perform our Christian actions day-in and day-out in spite of our formidable opposition? I think a key to the answer comes from Joe Dimaggio himself.

When asked near the end of his career why he still played so hard day after day, he said, "Because every day there is apt to be some child in the stands who has never before seen me play."

Let that sink into your conscience. Every day there is apt to be someone who has never before met Jesus Christ. And, their perception of Him just may come from my performance today.

"You are the light of the world. A city on a hill cannot be hidden. Neither do people light a lamp and put it under a bowl. Instead they put it on its stand, and it gives light to everyone in the house. In the same way, let your light shine before men, that they may see your good deeds and praise your Father in heaven."—Jesus Christ (Matthew 5: 14-16)

Father,
May we get on base today. Someone in the stands is watching for the very first time.
Through Jesus,
May it be.

A: Simon and Garfunkel (in the song, "Mrs. Robinson")

Week 22: The Summer Olympics

trivia

Q: What two famous assassinations took place in the same year as the 1968 Olympics?

"Great souls have wills, feeble ones have only wishes."—Chinese Proverb

I love the Summer Olympic Games.

It's hard to put your finger on what makes the Olympics so special. Maybe it's the athletes who compete for the sake of competition rather than seven figure salaries. Maybe it's the patriotic aspect, athletes giving all they have for country, a war without casualties. It could be the hints of world unification that makes the Olympic spirit special—citizens flying flags proudly while forming friendships with people from other cultures.

Whatever the case, one Olympic memory stands out above the rest. I didn't watch it personally; I only learned of it from a television special. The special featured past Olympic heroes, but the story I will never forget involved a runner whose name I have already forgotten. Let me tell you about his thrilling last-place finish.

The Summer Olympic Games of 1968 were held in Mexico City, Mexico. Many remember these games for Bob Beamon's destruction of the long jump record in his first jump ever in an Olympic competition, leaping almost two feet further than the old record. Others remember the games for Al Oerter's record-setting feat in the discus, winning at age thirty-two the gold medal for the fourth consecutive time. However, I will now remember these games for a last-place finisher in the marathon from Tanzania.

This hero from east-central Africa was not necessarily the worst runner in the race. What caused him to finish approximately an hour-and-a-half behind the gold medal winner from Ethiopia was an injury. During the twenty-six mile, three-hundred-eighty-five yard race, he dislocated his knee, sprained his ankle, and suffered two deep cuts on his leg. After bandaging the wounds, he resumed his quest for the stadium. His face grimaced with pain on each step. Darkness had descended when he finally entered the stadium midst the cheers of the thousands of fortunate spectators. With expressions of pain but not of disappointment, the new Olympic legend finally crossed the finish line.

On the television special, Olympic expert Bud Greenspan said he had the chance to speak with the runner twelve years later. He stated that he told the Olympian how much he had inspired the world with his determination, but had to ask why he did it. Why did he keep going when there was no prize at the end? Greenspan described the look the runner gave to him as one of disbelief. He stated, "Mr. Greenspan, my country did not send me five-thousand miles across the world to begin a race. They sent me to finish it."

What a beautiful thought.

God admires perseverance. Think of all the stories. The life of Job, Noah and the ark, Abraham waiting for his nation, Joseph in slavery, Joshua and the Jericho walls, Jacob working for Rachel, David as a fugitive, Daniel in a lion pit, Ruth with Naomi, and of course, Jesus on a cross. God honors those who make it to the finish line. It doesn't matter what place they arrive or what injuries have struck along the way; He just wants each one to be able to state as Paul did, that we "have finished the race."

I've noticed a disturbing trend in church. I've seen many people retire. I realize that health concerns and factors that I am not aware of come into play in the making of such decisions. Nonetheless, I wonder about the message it sends to those of us who are younger. Is the Christian race something we finish here on earth? Can we put in our years of service and then retire to the countryside? I know where Paul stood when he wrote those words to Timothy. He was planning a retirement party of sorts that involved decapitation for following Christ. No fishing trip, no golf lessons, no place up on the lake. Paul's retirement from active duty involved an executioner.

I don't write in accusation. I just hope we all see our Christian race as a race that's finish line stands at death and not before. I pray that none of us will give up before we get there.

Father,
May we keep going with our eyes fixed only on Jesus.
Through His Name,
Amen

A: Robert Kennedy and Dr. Martin Luther King, Jr

Week 23: Clutch Hitters

trivia

Q: In what year did the San Francisco Examiner publish Ernest Lawrence Thayer's poem, "Casey at the Bat?"

Consistency:
It's the jewel worth wearing;
It's the anchor worth weighing;
It's the thread worth weaving;
It's the battle worth winning.
—Charles R. Swindoll

Summer calls to the fore many aspects of American culture, not the least of which is baseball.

As Americans gather around barbecue grills, America's favorite pastime often wends its way into the festivities one way or another. It may be a simple game of catch or possibly a light-hearted game of wiffle ball. It may turn out to be a full-fledged pick-up game in the backyard. It might even end up in a trip to watch the big boys play.

No matter what, baseball is as much a part of summer life in America as mosquitoes and swimming pools.

Without waxing too philosophical, baseball is not only a part of life, but it also teaches its lessons, too. While eating peanuts and cracker jacks and root, root, rooting for the home team may not sound too academic, the concepts of teamwork, competition, strategy, sacrifice, and knowing one's role on the team are rather important lessons for us all. Plus, we're all just trying to get home in the end anyway.

In addition to all that, however, a myth concerning the popular game may teach us an important lesson, too.

Here it is: There's no such thing as a "clutch hitter."

Baseball fans understand the concept of a "clutch hitter" in spite of Casey's unsuccessful whiff that led all Mudville into therapy. For baseball-deficient readers, the term refers to the guy you want up at bat when the game is on the line. This is the hitter that will come through for your team when the bases are loaded in the last inning of play and the other team is screaming for you to fail. You don't want just anybody at the plate in moments like that—you want your "clutch hitter." In fact, "Casey at the Bat" uses this common knowledge to surprise us with Casey's unthinkable failure.

But here's the deal: Statisticians have proven the concept of the "clutch hitter" to be a myth. There's simply no such thing.

Oh, there are guys who do well in "clutch" situations, but Bill James and his researchers at Stats, Inc. have determined who these guys are. Allen Barra and Alan Schwarz, sportswriters for the *Wall Street Journal*, described their findings this way: "What a hitter does in most clutch situations is pretty much what he does the rest of the time."

Is there a lesson in all this? You bet your sweet pine tar there is. When the going gets tough, I'll tell you whom you want in your corner. I'll tell you exactly who to put up at the plate when the game is on the line:

Put the man up who performs well when the going isn't tough.

The reflections for you and me are quite profound. Spiritual life doesn't turn out to be easier than staring down Eric Gagne in Dodger Stadium. In fact, at times I believe even I could hit a tater off of Gagne before I could straighten out the spiritual complications of life I sometimes face. But life in the ninth inning doesn't turn out to be much different than life in the fifth, or even the situations we faced in the first. In actuality, it turns out that I will do in the clutch just what I've been training myself to do all along.

Practice really does make perfect.

When we talk of our spiritual lives, how will we really perform when things get tough? It just may turn out to be the same way we've been performing all along.

Father,
May we prove consistent in our life's performance.
As Jesus said, may we pick up our cross "daily" and
follow You.
In His name,
Amen

A: 1888 (June 3rd)

Week 24: The Stalkers 

trivia

Q: How tall and how wide is a goal in soccer?

"Our love for God is tested by the question of whether we seek him or his gifts."—Ralph Washington Sockman

Have you ever been stalked? I don't know that I have. Have you ever stalked someone? Well, I'm guilty here. I stalked a guy one weekend with two teenage girls.

My daughter went through this stage where she was infatuated with soccer star, Landon Donovan. That infatuation prompted a birthday trip to Dallas with good friend, Marianne, in tow. We had great seats, on the ninth row behind his bench, and we even received a free Landon Donovan bobblehead doll at the game. The best part of the day, though, happened a few hours before game time; hence, the discussion on stalking.

First of all, you might be wondering why a dad would help his daughter stalk her famous heartthrob. The simple answer is that as long as my daughter is in love with someone thousands of miles away that does not know her name, I'm happy. When he knows our phone number, I'm a completely different person.

A simple e-mail to a soccer representative in Dallas landed the information on the hotel where he would be staying. A simple Internet search and I knew how to get there.

We made it to the hotel mid-afternoon, and we saw the team's chartered bus out in front. When we made it inside, the girls quickly discovered the team eating their pre-game meal in a meeting room. After they stared at the guys a while, the guys shut the door. We then tried to play it cool. We took our seats in the lobby and casually perused the *Dallas Morning News*, appearing interested in its content. Before long, the team marched out of the meeting room and headed up to their rooms. We waited for a while, expecting they would be back down soon, but when they didn't show, my two teenage stalkers began working the elevators. They eventually met some of the players and had a nice conversation with the coach of the San Jose Earthquakes. I kept reading the paper.

After quite some time, the players began to make their way down toward the lobby, and a few congregated by the bar. My brave teenage companions decided to wander over close to the players, and after catching their attention, ask if they could have their pictures made with them. I peeked from behind the newspaper. Things did not go exactly as planned. When they made their approach and asked their question, Landon Donovan appeared out of nowhere and agreed to have his picture made with them. They acted cool, saving any drool until they got back into my car.

Later that night at the game, we scoffed at all the little kids with their Landon Donovan jerseys. "They weren't hanging out with him this afternoon, were they?" we'd say, with our arrogant little laughs. People will go to great lengths to get close to someone famous. Listen to me, sounding all innocent. I'll do it, too!

Do we feel that way about God?

Many of the Psalms betray authors infatuated with God. Psalm 42:2: "My soul thirsts for God, for the living God. When can I go and meet with God?" The verse before says, "As the deer pants for streams of water, so my soul pants for you, O God."

Or consider what David wrote in the Judean wilderness in Psalm 63: "God — you're my God! I can't get enough of you! I've worked up such hunger and thirst for God, traveling across dry and weary deserts. So here I am in the place of worship, eyes open, drinking in your strength and glory. In your generous love I am really living at last! My lips brim praises like fountains. I bless you every time I take a breath; My arms wave like banners of praise to you." (MSG)

Is that the way you think about God? Maybe I'm just a cynic, but it seems like we are more consumed with how many times we have to go to church, how often we ought to be reading our Bibles, and how much time I should have spent in prayer.

Like I said, I will go to great lengths to get close to someone I want to see. I ask you as I ask myself: Do we really want to be close to God?

Father,
You are my hero, and You willingly grace me with
Your Presence. May my desire to just be close to You
always be strong.
With devotion,
Amen

A: Eight feet tall, and eight yards wide

Week 25: That's A Winner!

trivia

Q: What season was Jack Buck's first as "play-by-play man" for the St. Louis Cardinals?

"Christianity spread rapidly during the first century because all Christians saw themselves as responsible for disseminating the gospel."—Erwin W. Lutzer

June 18, 2002: The opening line of the AP wire read, "One of most distinctive voices in sports has been silenced." Jack Buck, legendary broadcaster, had died at age seventy-seven.

For a lifelong St. Louis Cardinal baseball fan like me, the loss was significant. Strangely enough, though I never spoke with Mr. Buck personally, I felt as if a part of me died with him. It was not a loss contained to Cardinal fans, however. Jack Buck, and his gravel-voice, covered seventeen Super Bowls and many Monday Night Football games for CBS radio, plus a couple of years as the lead baseball announcer for CBS.

But the baseball Cardinals was his life.

He began as Harry Caray's sidekick back in 1954, and for nearly fifty years, Buck relayed the highs and lows of each season to his loyal radio listeners. With each victory, his scratchy voice would utter his signature line, "That's a winner!" And for every significant event, he seemed to know exactly what to say.

In 1987, when Ozzie Smith shocked everyone with his first left-handed home run to win Game 5 of the NL Championship Series, he shouted, "Go crazy, folks, go crazy!" Every Cardinal fan did, and his words etched permanent memories for all of us.

In 1998, Jack Buck was there every step of the way as Mark McGwire chased Roger Maris' home run record. When McGwire finally tied Maris and the crowd noise exploded over the airwaves, Jack Buck calmly stated, "Pardon me for a moment while I stand and applaud."

Every listener felt as if Jack Buck was a trusted friend. He was a Hall of Fame broadcaster literally, but he achieved that ranking for more than just his record of accomplishments. As a broadcaster, he was the epitome of class.

I simply want to tell you today that every Christian should see a role model in Jack Buck.

You see Jack Buck never swung a baseball bat in the major leagues. He never threw a pitch, recorded an out, or managed a team. He never claimed ownership of a major league franchise, or even spent time working his way up through the minors. And yet, his death was a headline event for one reason: He brought the game to the people.

With dependability and with class, he bridged the gap between the excitement of the big leagues and the mundane lives of the common fan.

Christians have no claims on being God. Christians have no claims on perfection. And when it comes down to it, I cannot save anyone from his or her sins. Come to think of it, I can't even do that for myself. I can do one thing, however. I can bring the game to others. With dependability and with class, I can at least do that. I can bring the "good news" of God to the lives of the common man.

I've never thought about it before, but I guess the name "broadcaster" would be a good term for a Christian to emulate. To cast the "good news" out in a broad manner. To let as many folks that our voice can reach know about Jesus. That's a pretty good job description for all of us.

And when we do it well, I guess we can say in the words of the late, great Jack Buck .... "That's a winner!"

Father,
We can only do so much. We are not very good players. And yet, may we do what we can. May we bring Your message to a world waiting eagerly to hear. May we do so with class.
All asked through the authority of Jesus,
Let it be.

A: 1954

Week 26: Lance Armstrong

trivia

Q: How many of his multiple Tour de France victories did Lance Armstrong win before being diagnosed with testicular cancer?

"If my testimony makes anyone wish to emulate me, it is a mistaken testimony; it is not a witness to Jesus."—Oswald Chambers

ESPN Classic is the greatest television channel in the history of mankind. Okay, that may be a bit overdramatic, but I really like it anyway. My favorite ESPN Classic show is *Sports Century*, a show that takes a biographical look at some prominent figure from the world of sports. The presentation is honest. As you are ushered behind the scenes, you see the good, bad, and the ugly of a life of fame.

I remember one episode in particular when ESPN Classic presented the life of Lance Armstrong.

Admittedly, I know little about cycling. I can still ride a bicycle (I think). I cannot ride a bicycle very fast or for very long, much less both at the same time. Lance Armstrong has made history by doing just that combination.

Even more amazing than his record setting victories in the most famous bike race of them all, the Tour de France, Armstrong overcame testicular cancer to do so. We fellas cringe just saying the words. Imagine how we'd cringe finding ourselves face-to-face with the illness. For Lance Armstrong, at the height of his illness, doctors gave him a

50/50 chance of survival. He has done much more than survive. He has become an amazing sports champion.

He encountered skeptics when he emerged from intense chemotherapy sessions, resumed his cycling passion, and then began to win. The European cycling community in particular felt his cancer had been some sort of hoax. They felt that way because his performance was too amazing to be true. What Lance Armstrong did was impossible it seemed. Larger than life.

ESPN Classic reported that the greatest cyclist of all time said that many people tried to get him to give credit to God for what happened in his life. He refused. He said that he overcame cancer and reached the pinnacle of cycling glory, not because of God, but because he worked his butt off—harder than anyone else.

How do you like them apples?

I, for one, admire his honesty. I believe there is a Creator of all that takes issue with Lance Armstrong. I will let the two of them have their own conversations.

I am most interested in the people who tried to get him to give credit to God.

On one hand, there are the folks who truly want God to receive the glory for what He has done in this world. I'm all right with them.

I think there's another hand, though. I suspect there are people who want him to give credit to God for selfish reasons—to make them believe in some way. For that group, I am glad Armstrong gave the answer he gave. There is a choice for all of us to make, you see, and a choice indicates two sides. This particular sports champion promotes the alternative.

It all comes down, it seems, to a faith decision. Will I believe in a Creator? Or not .... Some offer up the achievements of humanity as just that, while others see in human history only the grace of God. The choice is up to you.

There are proponents for each side. Our decision, however, is not based on the testimony of man; that is just fodder for our faith choice. In the end, we make our decisions only in our hearts.

What have you decided?

Father,

May our faith not rest in human testimony, but in the life of Jesus Christ.

Through Him,

Amen

A: Zero

FALL

Fall is classic.

It appears on Friday night in small towns all across America with a cool breeze under bright lights. Twangy hometown announcers mumble across scratchy public address systems while high school drummers announce the beginning of football season. It seems entire towns turn out to stand around drinking Dr. Pepper out of paper cups and talk about their chances this year. Sixteen-year-old boys, pumped to a fever pitch by slobbering coaches, crash out of the locker room and feel like heroes.

Those adolescent boys dream of playing on Saturday afternoons, where the bands are better, the stadiums are legendary, and the majorettes are college girls. They long to charge out of tunnels in places like Happy Valley or Death Valley. They dream of life in college towns like Tuscaloosa or South Bend, or of being a Longhorn or a Cornhusker. Most never will, but they begin turning into men just thinking about it.

The college heroes dream, too, but they dream instead of playing on Sundays, where the bands turn into productions, the stadiums are known by corporate sponsors, and the cheerleaders have now become women. When the Bears head up to Green Bay, or the Cowboys ride into Washington, or Oakland climbs to Denver, football reaches it's zenith. Young men long for it. It happens every fall.

But the actual "classic" of fall comes in two baseball stadiums every October. American heroes appear here in the bottom of the ninth of game sevens with everything on the line. The leaves have turned colorful, and everyone else with good sense has changed to uniforms requiring facemasks and shoulder pads (or gone to games played indoors), but two baseball teams still play a summer game in October. Their bullpen pitchers wear parkas, and their hitters blow into their hands to take the sting off when wood meets rawhide, and millions of people around the world watch to see who will rule the world. One hundred sixty-two regular seasons games plus the playoffs plus a World Series adds up to one team left standing when fall comes to a close.

Basketball launches its season in the fall in high school gyms, on college campuses, and in professional arenas. Dick Vitale reappears on television showing no need for antidepressants. Midnight Madness celebrates the season's birth in places like Cameron Indoor Stadium, and down the road in Chapel Hill. Across the country, at Pauley Pavilion, the very gym tells a story of Coach.

Talladega races every fall, too. The Superspeedway in Alabama claims to be the biggest, fastest, most competitive racetrack in existence. To NASCAR fans, it is a spiritual pilgrimage. 15,000 people live in Talladega, Alabama, where there are 143,000 seats at the track, not to mention thousands of spaces on a 212-acre infield. When the Winston 500 approaches, race-hungry fans begin showing up a full week before the roar of the race begins. NASCAR fan or not, Talladega in the fall is classic.

And fall is the time of year for a softball game. Softball transformed from a church league activity to a big business. Good athletes with factory jobs get their glory day fixes now from nights at the softball fields in intense competition. They invest in expensive bats, carry them in their bat bags, and hold on to their athletic prowess as long as they possibly can. In the fall, they and their wives carry their chairs, bug spray, and sun block to public fields all over the nation for team trophies and personal pride.

Fall is volleyball season, too. While the guys play football, girls sweat in hot gyms digging hard spikes in the back row and practicing their serves. Some of the most thrilling comebacks in all of sports occur in those high school gyms on Tuesday nights with only few witnesses in one of the toughest, fastest, and most athletic sports of them all. Setters run miles each night in twenty-foot intervals with their eyes and hands toward the ceiling, and blockers extend high above the net hoping to reject the fury of the coming attack. Few come to watch. They are the lucky ones.

Something else occurs in the fall, too. Time changes. More than just the colors of the leaves and the temperature of the air—the very clock changes when Daylight Savings Time ends. And the night comes closer. Time changes, and we head indoors to reflect on a nearly spent year. It is darker and colder now, yet still quite colorful.

Yes, fall is a classic time of year.

When life brings reflection.

Week 27: Backyards

trivia

Q: Which future hall-of-famer had his own "field of dreams" built for him by his dad when growing up on a farm in Van Meter, Iowa?

"We live less than the time it takes to blink an eye, if we measure our lives against eternity .... I learned a long time ago that a blink of an eye in itself is nothing. But the eye that blinks, that is something. A span of life is nothing. But the man who lives that span, he is something. He can fill that tiny span with meaning, so its quality is immeasurable though its quantity may be insignificant."—Chaim Potok

As a child, I loved my backyard. It was long and narrow, which made for perfect football games with friends. With a little imagination, it was also well suited for some killer wiffle ball games.

In my memory, on our back sidewalk with a panoramic view of it all, I notice the old, rusty swing set close on my left with my little tree house just behind it. It wasn't much of a tree house, just some wire mesh nailed up in a tree for a place to sit. A long metal pole ran up from the ground next to my wire seat, another creation of my dad's to satisfy my temporary Batman craze with a Batpole. A little further away, still on my left, were two trees. I still remember the day my dad and I planted them. Although I probably wasn't over six years old, I was taller than both the plum and silver maple trees. I outgrew them for a while, but they eventually towered over everything, including me.

To my right, just east of home plate stood my dunk goal. I never could jump, but the eight-foot high goal allowed me to do my Dr. J impersonations anyway. No grass grew in the immediate area around the dunk goal, a result of too many days out with my old basketball. A huge catalpa tree stood midway through the yard on the right-hand border (a.k.a. first base). Forty or fifty feet tall, it stood as a challenge for me to top it with my football punts and my baseball arm. It wasn't easy, but I could eventually do it. An old tire swing also hung from the catalpa tree, a useless tire my dad had painted white. I can still feel the breeze as I swung back and forth on a cool autumn afternoon.

At the back of the "yard" was a ditch. As a child, it was a huge ditch. Later on, it turned out to be two or three feet deep. On the left hand side, there were two crossties that served as a bridge to the other side. On the right hand side, a rope swing dangled from a sturdy limb, offering round-trip transportation, too. As I grew, of course, a good running leap also landed me on the other side to return my heroic punts and home runs.

In the space in between, the heart of the yard, was our golf course. Four primitive holes criss-crossed the yard, dug out with spoons and planted with empty cans of corn. We owned one golf club (a four-iron) that served as driver, pitching wedge, and putter for us all. My dad still owns the course record with an unbelievable eight (four under par).

I miss our backyard.

I thought about it in particular when my mom came to visit us once. I had remembered on occasion my mom putting around with our four-iron in the backyard, claiming that she would love to get out on a real golf course someday. Of course, neither of my parents ever did. So I took a vacation day that Monday and took her golfing. Shoulder problems prevented her from really playing, but she rode in the cart with me around a beautiful course on the Gulf. She took pictures of two alligators, one lurking the water, the other sunning on the bank. She stood out on the tee box, meandered down some fairways, and walked the greens. She held the flag for me when I would putt, and on several occasions when the Course Marshal was nowhere in sight, she did some putting herself. The years of putting in a bumpy backyard with a four-iron paid off. Given a real putter and a smooth green, she's pretty good.

I enjoyed my mother's smiles that day, but I still miss our bumpy backyard with its cheap tire swing, crosstie bridge, wire mesh tree house, and rope swing to the neighbor's yard. And I miss those breezes on lazy afternoons when the universe opened up for me in that long and narrow backyard. Every time I think about it, I smile.

Heaven will be a glorious reward. But I suspect when we're there and looking back, we will wistfully realize that the dreamy anticipation was pretty wonderful, too.

Father,
May our dreams of the beauty of Heaven not keep
us from appreciating this backyard.
In the name of Jesus,
Amen

A: Bob Feller

Week 28: Church Softball

trivia

Q: Instead of sixty feet, six inches, how far is the pitcher's mound from home plate in men's slow-pitch softball?

"We see actual things, and we say that we see them, but we never really see them until we see God; when we see God, everything becomes different. It is not the external things that are different, but a different disposition looks through the same eyes as the result of the internal surgery that has taken place."—Oswald Chambers

Our church softball season ended with three straight wins, thank you very much. In fact, we were on such a roll that the last two of those three wins came because the other teams didn't show up. That's because they were scared of us, right? That's the only thing that makes sense to me.

Church softball was a good thing for us. We had fun together, and some of us even grew closer to one another along the way.

But I have to admit that enjoying softball was a challenge for me. I am not very good, and I make it a habit to avoid things like that. Personal problem, I'm sure, but it is downright embarrassing to go out in public and make a fool of yourself.

Since I actually enjoy public speaking (and that is the number one fear to many), it may be a pretty good analogy to have those who feel weak there imagine hooking up with a public speaking team that performs every Saturday night. If you would run far away, that is sometimes how I felt.

Nonetheless, softball was still fun. It was interesting to watch all of us get older and have a more difficult time doing things we used to be able to do naturally.

I heard a story from an adult softball team of a man who was considerably older than the rest of his team, but just could not give up the sport. During one game, the old timer was playing third base when a line drive screamed over his leap and outstretched glove. At the end of the inning, on the way back to the bench, the left-fielder caught up with the third baseman, held his thumb and index finger a couple of inches apart and said, "That much."

The older third-baseman nodded his head and said, "Yeah, I know. I almost had it."

His younger teammate replied, "No. I mean that's how far you got off the ground."

Sports can at least show us that the body does slow down with time. It serves as a literally painful reminder that time does roll on.

Shouldn't surprise us, though.

On one hand, physical exercise is a good thing. The Bible encourages us to do so: "Do you not know that your body is a temple of the Holy Spirit, who is in you, whom you have received from God? You are not your own; you were bought at a price. Therefore, honor God with your body."

On the other hand, though, we know that the flesh really is passing away—too quickly at times, it seems. It shouldn't get to us, though. In fact, it's a downright helpful reminder of a fact we too often forget.

You see, Paul (who said to honor God with your body) told Timothy that "...physical training is of some value, but godliness has value for all things, holding promise for both the present life and the life to come."

So, let your aching muscles remind you to invest some time in taking care of the body you have been given. However, most importantly, let them remind you that this body will pass away, and that all efforts toward godliness should receive the greatest attention.

Whether you suck at softball or not.

Father,
May we keep life in perspective.
In Jesus' Name,
Amen

A: Fifty feet

Week 29: Team Loyalty

trivia

Q: What was the score differential in the most lopsided game in MLB history?

"Teach us that no evil is intolerable but a guilty conscience, and that nothing can hurt us, if with true loyalty of affection, we keep thy commandments and take refuge in thee; through Jesus Christ our Lord. Amen."—William Ellery Channing

Sad, sad, sad ....

I have been a fan of the St. Louis Cardinals since at least 1979. Beginning that year, my family made a summer trip to Busch Stadium an annual event. That lasted from 1979 up until about 1998. Then, I moved to south Mississippi. Much to my dismay, I had not seen the Cardinals in person since.

However, when the 2003 season approached, I noticed that the Cardinals played a Friday night game at Houston in September, and I began to dream of it working out where I'd sneak over for a game in a hot pennant race. Not long afterwards, one of my church elders/heroes—the biggest baseball fan I know—said he would like to add Minute Maid Park in Houston to his collection of visited parks. I mentioned the Cards/Astros match-up in September. He told me to plan a trip and count him in. That's how it all started.

It turned out that eight of us fellers from church decided to make the trip over together, I the only Cardinals fan of the group. To protect my fellow church brothers ... well, more honestly, because I'm a chicken, I didn't sport any Cardinal colors. I went to the game incognito.

Every time I saw a Cardinals fan before the game, though, I struck up a conversation, revealing my true colors. I was excited. This was going to be great.

Then we got whooped.

I mean, we got whooped like a guest on the Jerry Springer Show. We got whooped like David Duke at a Tyson fight. It was ugly.

In my twenty-five years of watching baseball, I don't think I've ever seen a game so ugly. The Astros hit every Cardinal pitcher early and often. Their pitcher was crushing screaming line drives off our pitchers. Our hitters were useless. Our fielders couldn't pick up the ball. It was the Bad News Bears make it to the major leagues. It was embarrassing.

At some point, I became very thankful that I did not wear any official Cardinals merchandise. In some warped act of treason, I began to smile sadistically at humiliated fans wearing Cardinal red. I was the Benedict Arnold of baseball fans. I felt smug.

But I'm the loser here.

At least those true fans stuck by the team. Through thick and thin—well, it was pretty much thin the whole night—but they stuck by them the whole way. They took the humiliation. It was, after all, their team.

We Christians sometimes act a lot more like I did than we ought. We have a favorite team, and we feel quite a fondness for the side of Jesus Christ. We're rooting for His side to win. However, although He offers us a spot on the team, we quite prefer life as a spectator. More than that, we prefer life as an anonymous spectator. We'll just see how things go, and if they turn ugly, we'll be quite happy to be unnoticeable thank you very much.

But we're called to sport the colors.

Let's buy the t-shirts. Let's wear the hats. Let's stick by our team; through thick and thin, in good times and bad, 'til death do we part.

It will be worth it in the end.

You see, Jesus' team can even whoop up on the Astros.

Father,
May we not be ashamed of the Gospel ...
Through Jesus,
Amen

A: Twenty-five runs (when the Boston Red Sox defeated the St. Louis Browns 29-4 at Fenway Park on June 8, 1950)

Week 30: Coach Boone

trivia

Q: What was the actual score in the 1971 Virginia state high school football championship game when the T.C. Williams Titans defeated Andrew Lewis?

"To find his place and fill it is success for a man."— Phillips Brooks

Unleash the topic of "the greatest sports movie of all time," and you've opened a never-ending debate. I'll be with those of you who argue for *Remember the Titans*.

That movie is based on the true story of the 1971 T.C. Williams High School football team. A federal court order forced three rival high schools in Alexandria, Virginia, to merge. The drama came from the town's deep racial division. One of the schools was completely filled with African-Americans while another was 100% Caucasian. T.C. Williams had been about two-thirds "white" before the consolidation.

The greatest controversy came, however, when a black man named Herman Boone was named head football coach. Although Coach Boone had a proven track record, he was new to the school system and was chosen over a legendary white coach named Bill Yoast. The amazing story is how Coach Boone led his team to overcome their hatred for one another and become a powerful team, a team that leveled their competition with an undefeated state championship season.

I went with my friend Billy to hear Coach Herman Boone speak on the University of South Alabama's campus. THE Coach Boone (not Denzel Washington) was traveling around the country with his newfound fame, and, to be honest, the part where he presented his talk (more like a sermon) was a bit scattered. However, the question and answer session that followed his talk was more than worth the trip.

I had to roll my eyes at certain questions (like an obvious journalism student requesting his stance on affirmative action). There was also a football coach looking for some gridiron advice, but for the most part, most of us were enthralled by the movie, and we wanted to know what the real story was behind the Titans.

I was amazed to learn that the football team was even better than the movie portrayed, and that the horrible racism Coach Boone faced was even worse. He informed us that the brick thrown through his window in the movie was no brick in real life. It was human excrement. He told us that the referees who worked against him in one game in the movie worked against him all season. And unbelievably, some of Coach Boone's own assistant coaches would give his playbook to the teams they were to play in advance, hoping the Titans would lose so Coach Yoast could replace him. In response, Coach often gave his competition a second copy of his playbook, and the mighty Titans rolled on.

At one point Coach Boone stated, "You may ask me, 'How'd you not kill somebody? How did you keep your cool?' Let me tell you why—I truly feel I was given a torch. I was given a torch to carry so that others could follow where I lead."

I suggest this is why moviegoers loved the story. As my friend stated, there is something about "being a part of something greater."

I couldn't help but think about God that night, and the lip service we often pay to Him. We claim to believe, and we claim that He has some sort of purpose for us; yet I wonder if we truly believe that we have been given a torch in this world. I wonder if we truly believe we are made to be a part of something greater. In the setting of "church," we don't act like it very much. I'm not talking church attendance and things like that (although I believe Coach would say practice time is very important). Instead, I wonder if we intend on looking back at our lives to see if we carried the torch God handed us. I wonder if we even care to know what the torch is?

Maybe I'm sounding condescending. If so, I don't mean to. I'm actually being hard on myself. I guess I keep thinking that in many ways I have been called to a position similar to Coach Boone. I am to motivate a diverse group of people who may or may not have any plans on working together. I just pray that I can succeed even a little like he did.

But I'm not sure Tom Cruise is tall enough to play me in the movie.

Father,
May every one of us somehow recognize what level
of greatness You call us toward. May
we aspire to success in showing You to the world.
In His Name,
Amen

A: 27-0 (The Titans held Andrew Lewis to minus five total yards—sixty passing, and minus sixty-five rushing.)

Week 31: Unexpected Success

trivia

Q: What is the official height of the net for girl's high school volleyball?

"The secret of success is to do all you can without thought of fame."—Proverb

I learned to appreciate volleyball in high school. I went to a small school, and volleyball was practically the only sport available for girls. Our team was really good, but I suspect my interest in the sport stemmed less from the girls' talent and more from the fact that there were girls playing it.

So I knew a bit about the sport when my daughter began playing at the same school in fourth grade up until our move to the Mississippi Coast during her sixth grade year. To our great disappointment, volleyball wasn't so big here. There were no middle school programs. We decided we might have to learn to adjust to life without volleyball.

Erica didn't play in seventh grade, but in the eighth made the high school's junior varsity team. The coach was literally recruited the week school started, one week before the first game, and the sweet, young lady did not know anything about the sport. It turned out to be a long year. In ninth grade however, everything magically transformed.

Yes, I'm a proud (and biased) dad, but that Ocean Springs volleyball season was amazing. As far as I can tell, this volleyball program had never had a winning season—until that one, that is. At one point, after winning a first place battle against a powerful, experienced team, the Lady Greyhounds' record stood at ten wins and one loss. The one loss was against the team they defeated that night in a thrilling, three-game match.

It was really incredible. Like previous years, the new coach lacked volleyball experience. And like the previous year, he was hired one week before school started. The team that arrived to practice on day one came with very little experience as well, with nary a senior among them. All of this added up, of course, to promise another long season. "Building for the future" would be the logical goal. But someone forgot to tell the girls and the coach that they couldn't just go ahead and win anyway.

It was so much fun to watch that team discover its potential. They surprised themselves with each passing achievement, finding new joy each time. That year will always be my favorite. We expected to win afterwards. Expectations always come with success. In ninth grade, however, it was like Christmas coming in the middle of a hot, sweaty gymnasium. Each present was unexpected. Each startled smile priceless.

I heard that the entire high school (of over a thousand students) talked volleyball before that big first-place game that season. I witnessed a large, loud crowd that night including many fans, students, and teachers who had never been to a volleyball game. The middle school principal who had told the volleyball team and parents to "clean up his gym after we get finished with it" was actually there mopping the floor. Newspaper articles popped up regularly for a bunch of girls and a young coach who did not let the facts stand in the way of success.

Why don't the people of God accomplish more? Maybe we expect too much. Maybe each success is met with a "well, it's about time" response instead of the giggling joy of wide-eyed dreamers. Maybe we would do better to celebrate each accomplishment more, regardless of its size, and criticize each shortcoming less.

In 2nd John, verse 4, John wrote, "It has given me great joy to find some of your children walking in the truth ...." That's an odd statement. Shouldn't John have said that it gives him "some" joy to find "some" children walking in the truth? Wouldn't great joy come with all the children doing right?

Not if you listen to Jesus. Jesus told us that the narrow road would not be well attended. Jesus told us to expect a lot out of God, but quite honestly not to expect a lot out of those who claim to be walking toward Him. If we could change our expectations accordingly, celebrate more and criticize less, we might also begin to experience the wide-eyed joy and success that I witnessed in an amazing little volleyball team.

> *Father,*
> *May we drop our expectations of frail human beings. May we enjoy each small victory with the joy of a child, and in so doing, begin to experience greater triumph than we could even imagine.*
> *In the Name of Jesus,*
> *Amen*

A: Seven feet, four and 1/8 inches

Week 32: Y.M.C.A.

trivia

Q: Where was the first Y.M.C.A. established?

"For him who confesses, shams are over and realities have begun."—William James

I know I'm a broken record, but … I started working out again. Yeah, yeah, yeah, I know I've said that before, but this time I'm serious about it. Okay, I've said that before, too, but humor me anyway. This time, my entire family is serious about physical fitness. I hope we can motivate one another.

We joined our local YMCA and entered the weight room. In my dreams, I pictured the scene as a new boxer enters an arena, with everyone stopping to stare. Well, the staring part came true, but it was more like when the Beverly Hillbillies moved into Beverly Hills. Oh well, you've got to start somewhere.

I felt as if I had a good attitude going into it this time. I'm woefully out of shape. I know it already, so pretending doesn't accomplish very much. I know that all of those men and women in the weight room with perfect bodies had to start somewhere, so I simply decided to swallow my pride and get started. I also knew that I could destroy myself quickly by trying to do too much too fast, so I determined to pace myself.

All of this sounds good, but it still wasn't very easy.

I rode an exercise bike for a while and tried out a few machines no one else seemed too interested in using. I wanted to use one machine in particular, but Hulk Hogan was using the machine next to it so I waited to preserve the dignity of my family name. Eventually, a couple of teenage boys started using the machine I wanted and Mr. Hogan moved on. I piddled around until the teenage boys left, and I nonchalantly walked over. I moved the weight down from one-twenty to sixty and prayed no one was watching. I prepared to embarrass myself when I noticed the two teenage boys coming back. One said, "Sir, I've got one more set to go. Can I finish?"

I said "No problem!" and the boys moved the weight back to their liking. He finished his set, looked at me and said, "Did you have it on sixty?" He only laughed at me with his eyes, which I very much appreciated. I said, "Yeah, whatever your great-grandma had it on earlier" to complete my humiliation.

But I'm going back anyway.

I guess I've been a loser a lot in my life, so it may come easier to me than others. But you know it may be my experience with God that makes this most possible. Peter wondered how many times he had to forgive his brother—seven times? Jesus replied that an infinitely higher number was more appropriate. At least that's how God deals with us.

Are you like me? Have you made the trip back to God with the same confession for the same sin more times than you care to admit? Have you wondered if you've reached your limit? If you've gone to the well one too many times?

I'm glad Jesus and Peter had their little discussion about the number of times you get a fresh start because I wonder, too. I don't know why God would give me as many new beginnings as He has. I don't deserve them. And yet, I remember reading a very good question in what I'm sure was one of Max Lucado's books (though I don't remember which one): What makes me think I deserved it the first time?

I'm headed back to that gym. I sure hope that it sticks this time around, and that I'll be the poster child for physical fitness. My track record would lead everyone to think that it won't work. Track records won't lead you to accomplish anything, though.

Our spiritual track record may not be a source of motivation either, but don't live life based on a track record. Jesus didn't come to say that with His help you could fail just like you were failing before. He said that anything was possible with Him on our side.

So start over again. Confess your sins again, and head back into the training room of life. You may think that you're fooling yourself, but don't listen. Humble yourself and start over. God will go to the gym with you.

Father,
Thank You for not laughing at us, but instead loving
and encouraging us to keep pressing on toward holiness.
In Jesus' name,
Amen

A: London, England (June 6, 1844)

Week 33: Loneliness

trivia

Q: In the lonely sport of cross-country, which NCAA school has the most Division I national championships?

"The soul hardly ever realizes it, but whether he is a believer or not, his loneliness is really a homesickness for God."—Hubert van Zeller

I attended a high school football game recently that pitted two very different teams against one another. I sat on the side of the small, private school. I found a place off to myself several rows behind a group of junior high students. Boys with shaggy haircuts and caps made to look like they are old (both in fashion now) flirted with girls sporting little purses and outfitted in the latest designer clothes. None of them recognized a football game was being played within a thousand miles. After the game, they joined with their parents in their respective luxury vehicles to head to their spacious homes.

And I felt out of place.

On the way out of the stadium after the game, I passed the other team. This team was happy after their commanding victory over their opponent, and they bounced and chanted in their excitement. The football team hails from an economically depressed, stereotypical part of Mississippi. As the little wide-eyed boys hovered around their high school heroes (none of which sported designer clothes), I saw a twinkle in their eyes. It was hope stemming from athletics. They dreamed of a day when football would bring them all the items their counterparts already had.

And I felt out of place.

I left the parking lot to drive home, and I traveled through the "bad" part of town. I passed by a run-down bar. You know the picture. A dismal building surrounded by a packed parking lot, lit by several neon signs advertising the alcoholic beverages found within. Several adults were staggering outside as I passed with crooked smiles on their faces and bottles in their hands. These folks did not drive luxury vehicles nor did they believe a sport would bring them worldly riches. Their hope for happiness now exists in the form of a bottle.

And I felt out of place.

My final observation came after I made it back to the main road. On my right, I passed three huge casinos. They stick out not only for their size, but also for the glittering lights that draw visitors from all over the world. People dreaming of the designer fashions and luxury vehicles and massive homes file inside the lights to see if they might be lucky after all. Some are. Most aren't.

And once again, I felt alone.

I crossed a bridge that night with an overwhelming sense of loneliness. Oh, I have a great family to go home to, so don't feel sorry for me. I also have a variety of friends in a variety of places, but that night I felt out of touch with everything. I felt alone.

Maybe God was giving me a gift that evening.

Dag Hammarskjold once prayed, "Didst thou give me this inescapable loneliness so that it would be easier for me to give thee all?" Maybe so. Maybe that's what I needed to feel.

Christianity brings individuals into community—with God as well as with one another. And yet we should remember that by its very nature it also brings along a type of loneliness. A realization of alien status. Feeling a stranger in your own hometown. Being able to sing that this world is not my home.

I guess on this earth every one of us is plagued with some form of loneliness. You may seek to fill this void with material possessions or with a bottle. Maybe you try both. I offer God as the answer. I offer God as the pathway to life, to joy, to peace, and to hope.

It's the very best I can do.

Father,
May I have shares of both loneliness and
community in all the necessary ways so I can keep
my focus on seeing You face to face someday.
Through the hope brought by Jesus,
Amen

A: The University of Arkansas at Fayetteville

Week 34: The Transfer Principle

trivia

Q: Of the millions of injury-related emergency room visits each year, approximately how many are sports-related?

"Do not follow where the path may lead. Go instead where there is no path and leave a trail."—Harold R. McAlindon

I went to college with a definite occupational goal in mind: I wanted to be a basketball coach. I decided to major in secondary education with an emphasis in social studies while taking just enough classes to gain my coaching certification, but make no mistake, my plan all along was to be the head man on the sidelines calling the shots.

I especially looked forward to the games. I loved imagining myself in heated situations. You know, three seconds on the clock, down by one, and we have the ball out-of-bounds under the basket. It's up to me to call the right play. That's what I dreamed about, and eventually it came true. Unfortunately, collegiate preparation for the coaching profession involved more than just "Last Second Play-Calling 101." I also had to take, "Care and Prevention of Athletic Injuries."

You must understand that I made good grades in school, but I never had any desire to be a doctor. Actually, I had no desire for any employment in any medical profession. Taking two aspirin was about the extent of what I wanted to know about medical care, and yet, coaches must learn the basics of preventing and caring for injuries.

The class I took was filled mostly with athletic trainers who already knew everything there was to know about the subject; they just had to go through the course for credit. And then there was Doug and myself. Our instructor labeled us "the coaches." (I believe we were called "the morons" by the trainers.) We received a LOT of individual attention, and we got the privilege of staying after class sometimes to make sure we really understood what was going on.

Even though we were "just coaches," we learned a lot. Learning how to tape an ankle sure came in handy in the next few years, and believe it or not, a lot of the medical jargon stuck somewhere in the recesses of my mind. Medical care was actually somewhat interesting.

For instance ....

There was one rehabilitative principle that I remember called something like "the transfer principle," though I'm sure its actual name is much more impressive. Here's what it basically states: if you have a leg that is injured so badly that it is immobilized, and if you extensively train the good leg, then some of the strength gained will transfer to the immobilized limb and help in the recovery process.

Pretty cool, huh?

Well, at least I thought it was cool. Even though it makes no medical sense, strengthening your left leg can help your right.

I know this concept is true, not because of any athletic training experiences I encountered, but because I once went to church with a man named Brad Gregg.

Brad became my friend at a time that I needed it. He came with spirit and devotion to God, and as I watched him at work, it changed me. Not once did Brad tell me that I needed to get my lazy hind end up off the church pew and out into the world, but that's the effect his energy had on me. His influence was strong.

I don't know about you, but there's been a time or two in my life when I've been on the excited end, and the spiritual lethargy surrounding me left me very frustrated. I was the living section of a nearly comatose body. In those times, the tendency was to be despondent over all "those" body parts that "ought to be" doing so much more.

Instead, I needed to remember that it was me that was slowing things up. Instead of frustration, maybe the answer to it all was for me to work out harder than ever.

At least that's the way it worked with me through Brad.

Learning about the body can be a difficult chore, I'm telling you. Being a part of one can be, too.

Father,
May You send us inspiration when we need it, and
may we be the inspiration the rest of the time.
Through Jesus,
Amen

A: 10%

Week 35: Playing With Pain

trivia

Q: How many points did Willis Reed score in his famous comeback in Game Seven of the 1970 NBA Finals?

"Pain is no evil, unless it conquer us."—Charles Kingsley

Rarely does my oldest daughter encourage me to write about her, so I am taking full advantage of her permission this time. As I have already written, Erica's freshman volleyball season was borderline miraculous. A new coach, some new players, and a new attitude led to something new for us—a winning season, and a trip to the state playoffs. Her sophomore year was nearly a repeat performance. This time, the team made it to the Elite Eight in the state of Mississippi, and at the team's year-end banquet, the coach named Erica the co-MVP of the team.

Then, half the team and the coach moved away.

Eleventh grade turned out to be not so bad, though. The new coach had been a volleyball connoisseur for much of his life. There were lots of good girls on the team, many good parents in the stands, and another trip to the post-season. Overall, things were good. One game in particular, however, stands out in my mind.

We were playing our first conference game against the St. Martin Yellowjackets. After winning a close first game 15-13, we were being whipped in game two. During that game, a hard hit from the opposition went toward my daughter's face in the back row. As usual, she reacted well, with both hands up for an overhead pass. However, for really the first time in seven years of volleyball, the ball hit wrong, badly jamming her right thumb. Tears arrived quickly, but play continued.

I'm the team's scorekeeper, and I immediately pointed it out to the coach. He had noticed, too, but the play continued. After a few volleys, the ball came back to Erica who was able to pass with her arms to keep the play alive. That brought more tears. I was hurting by now, but the play kept going.

Later, in this seemingly endless rally, the ball came back to Erica (who later told me thought her thumb was broken). It came at her face again, requiring another overhead pass to keep the play alive. She cringed, put up her hands, and made another good pass, sending new waves of pain through her body. More tears—some from me this time.

The play finally ended. Coach took Erica out of the game and had her put her hand in an ice chest. It was thankfully not broken, but a bad "jam" instead. The team ended up winning the match in three games, and of course, a few days later Erica's thumb was much improved and ready for the next opponent. It didn't slow her down very long.

It did slow me down—long enough for a very important lesson.

I think we're all playing injured. Not a one of us is innocent. Not a one of us is whole. We are playing with constant pain. And how we play tells a lot about our character. We could walk away from the game. That's always an option, I guess. It's kind of hard to walk away from life, but scores of folks check themselves out of the game anyway. We could lie down and cry. In fact, many do. Overwhelmed with our own sense of pain, and oblivious of the team that surrounds us, we may choose to form a one-man huddle and focus completely on what hurts us so deeply.

Or, we could do like my daughter, of whom I am very proud. We could keep the play alive, for the team of humanity of which we are a part. We could blink back the tears, fight through the pain, and when the play comes our way, be willing to endure the searing pain long enough to give our team a chance to survive.

Yes, we could do that.

Yes, I could do that.

Maybe I can play my role in life with as much courage as my daughter plays her sport. That would be quite an accomplishment.

Father,
Take us out of the game when You see fit, but while we're on the floor, we want to give You all we've got—for the good of the team.
Through Jesus,
Amen

A: Four

Week 36: Blind Bowling

trivia

Q: What is the age of the youngest player ever to roll a perfect 300 game?

"If you would hit the mark, you must aim a little above it; every arrow that flies feels the attraction of the earth."—Henry Wadsworth Longfellow

In grade school, for every field trip, my class had to choose between skating and bowling. I was a horrible skater, so I always voted for bowling. I always lost. But somewhere along the way, I had a few chances to hang out at the bowling alley. I'd search for the eight-pound ball that I could actually lift, and I'd put on those stylish shoes and try my best impression of Earl Anthony. I usually looked more like Earl Weaver.

It was fun nonetheless. For a few months during my senior year, my friend Scott and I made regular trips to the bowling alley during another one of our fleeting hobby interludes. We were okay, but nothing to write home about.

One night in college, however, I approached bowling nirvana. In Fayetteville, Arkansas, the local bowling alley tapped into the college atmosphere by promoting "Rock 'n Bowl" on Friday nights. For five bucks, you bowled for two hours, from midnight to 2am. The lights were turned down, rock videos blasted on a large screen, and an iced-down traveling keg of beverages made its way up and down the lanes offering its contents for sale. It was at Rock 'n Bowl that I achieved the apex of my bowling career.

It was sort of ironic, I guess, that the largest majority of the patrons that night were so inebriated that only I knew how good I was bowling, but the pins just kept falling. I wasn't sure how I was doing because (though it was new to me), when you have that many strikes and spares in a row, your score remains mostly a mystery.

But after the last frame, I checked out my score. I wasn't sure whether to rejoice or cry. I bowled a 199. One stinking pin short of a 200 game. I blamed it on the fact that I'm legally blind in my left eye, wondering if that provided some sort of a one-pin handicap, but somewhere in the world, Cee Cee Clark laughed at my request of the bowling gods.

In an amazing feat, she, at age fifty-four-year and legally blind in both eyes, threw twelve strikes in a row! That's a perfect three hundred game for all of you scoring at home. Now a perfect three hundred is an exceptional accomplishment, but it is downright amazing for someone who uses a Seeing Eye dog.

"I was so nervous throwing that last ball, I could barely let it go," she said. "When I heard everyone in the bowling alley explode, I knew I had my perfect game!"

The news report claimed that this grandmother from Virginia developed her love for bowling before her eyesight faded away. After her tragic loss, she learned to use her sense of touch to identify the back of the lane. She memorized the precise number of steps required in her approach, and as a result, joined the ranks of bowling perfection.

Now I am very proud of my 199 (and don't forget it came with my being legally blind in my left eye). But let's compare: 199 with one good eye versus 300 with zero good eyes. Okay, I lose. But I bet she was getting pointers from that Seeing Eye dog. I can't imagine bowling a perfect game in the first place, much less if I was blind. Cee Cee Clark's story definitely goes to prove that we can achieve all sorts of great things, overcoming huge obstacles, if we simply set our minds to them.

I started thinking about this specific story, and how it parallels Christian life.

Paul once wrote, "We live by faith, not by sight." Jesus said, "Be perfect, therefore, as your heavenly Father is perfect." Combined, the Bible teaches that God asks for a perfect game from blind people. That's the fact, Jack.

We're sure quick to justify our imperfections, though, and settle for less. God, here's what I have to offer: 199 with one good eye. That doesn't seem to be good enough, though. Jesus instead offers us a seemingly unattainable goal, not for constant frustration, but for constant challenge. Anything less than the best is simply not enough.

Blind perfection, huh? Ask Cee Cee Clark. It isn't impossible. Not if you set your mind to it.

> *Father,*
> *May our goals be far beyond our sight.*
> *Through Jesus,*
> *Amen*

A: Ten (Josey LaRocco, in Louisville, on February 14, 1998)

Week 37: Game Seven

trivia

Q: Bill Mazeroski is the only player in history to win a Game Seven of a World Series with a walk-off home run. Who threw the pitch?

"Far better it is to dare mighty things, to win glorious triumphs, even though checkered by failure, than to take rank with those poor spirits who neither enjoy much nor suffer much because they live in the gray twilight that knows not victory nor defeat."—Theodore Roosevelt

The infielders were in to make the force play at the plate. The outfielders were brought in some as well in the event of a sacrifice fly. The bases were loaded in the bottom of the ninth in a tied seventh game of the World Series, and Luis Gonzales stepped to the plate to face Mariano Rivera.

Gonzales, Arizona's best hitter, dug in against Rivera, the Yankees' best pitcher. Rivera opened with a strike. Then, with tensions mounting, the pinstriped closer offered his 0-1 pitch.

Gonzales swung and made contact.

Time stopped to watch the ball bloop into centerfield for a base hit, and Luis Gonzales suddenly achieved every baseball player's ultimate dream and became a World Series hero.

Every sport has its heroes that have come through in the clutch. Baseball has Bobby Thomson and Bill Mazerowski. Basketball has Michael Jordan and Larry Bird. Football has quarterbacks like Doug Flutie, Roger Staubach , John Elway, and as bad as it hurts for me to remember, that blasted Dwight Clark/Joe Montana connection.

I've been wondering, though: what is it that is so special about these heroes?

To be honest, Luis Gonzales' single was not that impressive. He had not fared well at the plate in the World Series. This man hit fifty-seven home runs during one season, and it now turns out that his most famous hit will be a weak single that barely made it out of the infield. What was so special about that?

He came through when it mattered.

Every baseball player's dream is to do what Gonzales did, but ironically every baseball player's nightmare is simply walking to the plate in his situation, too. All of the pressure. All eyes on you. You will be the "goat" if you strikeout. And yet, he calmly walked to the plate and delivered.

Lucius Annaeus Seneca lived at the time of Christ. He is quoted as saying, "'Tis nothing for a man to hold up his head in a calm; but to maintain his post when all others have quitted their ground and there to stand upright when other men are beaten down is divine."

That is heroism.

Tim Hansel once said, "The Bible is a first-hand story of goose-bump courage in very ordinary people who were invaded by the living God." When you think of it that is true. Joseph in Egypt. Moses before Pharaoh. Joshua and Caleb. David versus Goliath. Elijah on Mount Carmel. The 1st Century martyrs.

Jesus.

Sports often serve as a microcosm for life, and Luis Gonzales' performance in that memorable Game Seven serves well. In the long run, baseball games won't really matter, and yet, the courage to step up to the plate and deliver when the game is on the line—risking dramatic failure—that is what life is all about.

Thank God He's on our side.

Father,
May we have real faith so that we come through in the crunch for You.
In Jesus' name,
So be it

A: Ralph Terry

Week 38: Revenge

trivia

Q: In what year was the National Alliance for Youth Sports founded?

"The advice 'bomb them back to the Stone Age' may show that the speaker is already there himself, but it could, if followed, force all of us to join him."
—Robert F. Kennedy

I witnessed one morning quite possibly the epitome of the word "stupidity." In short, I observed parents at a soccer game for kids under the age of ten.

Now, I refuse to stereotype completely. You see I was also a parent of one of those entertaining youngsters. I was (and am) a parent with many, many faults of my own. Thankfully, one of those specific faults does not include a bulging vein in my neck from screaming at little kids and other, equally immature, parents (I use the word "parent" loosely for communication purposes only).

Before you say it, I am also aware that my faults lie closer to the judging discussion Jesus offers shortly after the instructions to turn the other cheek. But that's not my point right now.

I wonder why we even bother discussing what's wrong with the world? Is it any wonder that bloody homicides litter each evening's news? Why are we surprised when a person is accused of killing his spouse? Does a mother killing her own children really catch us off guard?

The world screams verbs like "take" and "hit" and "hurt" while Jesus offers "give" and "turn" and "help." At the coffee shops, we say, "What's this world coming to? How did we get in such a mess?"

I think I discovered the origins of the mess this morning on a soggy soccer field.

Surely, I jest. How could a parent screaming to her son, “If he kicks you again, KICK HIM BACK!” end up with a young man dead in a neighborhood fight? Or even more absurd, how could one parent taunting another with, “You’re the one that started it!” teach children anything that would lead to problems in the world?

I’m afraid that I am serious, though.

Where does revenge lead? Child abuse. Barroom brawls. Drive-by shootings. Assassinations. Terrorist attacks. Embezzlement. Adultery. Church splits. Broken friendships. Ahab. Jezebel. Haman. Herodias. Maybe even a crucifixion?

Revenge for what? Being taken advantage of. Having a different opinion. Jealousy. Failure. Guilt. Maybe just being born. Does it really matter, though, why human beings crave revenge? Instead, I think what the world really craves—or at least should crave—is some type of solution to the horrible effects of this dreadful disease.

“Do to others as you would have them do to you.” “Love one another as I have loved you.” The answer is so simple that it is almost painful to admit. Is it true?

If you want to know who wins in the war of revenge, I’d suggest a reading of Charles Darwin. On the other hand, if you’re interested in learning the final outcome from that silly notion of “turning the other cheek,” you could research Gandhi and Dr. King a little bit, too.

Overall, though, I’d suggest taking a look at Jesus. Yes, I suggest Jesus.

Father,
May we consider the long-term consequences of our
actions, and may we come to define “long-term”
in ways longer that go beyond how I feel at the
moment.
Through the example and promise of Jesus,
Amen

A: 1981

Week 39: Tiger Bait

trivia

Q: As of 2004, who holds the all-time lead in the head-to-head football match-up between LSU and Arkansas (the Battle of the Boot)?

"Football incorporates the two worst elements of American society: violence punctuated by committee meetings."—George Will

I am an Arkansas Razorback fan. I cannot recall when it started; some would say it occurred naturally via birth in the state of Arkansas. A few would disagree.

During my first year of college, I made my first trip to Fayetteville with my friends Deron and David. It was homecoming, and the Southwest Conference title was on the line against Texas A&M. We went without tickets, and miraculously found some on the fourth row, fifty-yard line behind the Razorback bench at face value! My love affair deepened that day. In fact, I transferred to the U of A that very next year and made it a point to be at every single home football game. I loved every one.

Since my graduation in 1992, my attendance dropped off. I made a few trips before moving to Mississippi, but since that move, a Razorback game has been a rare treat. I have only seen four games in person during that time, all against the LSU Tigers.

In 1999, LSU had a horrible year. The Razorbacks were rocking. I went to Death Valley to watch the match-up. They kicked our behinds all over Baton Rouge.

In 2001, I went back. This time, my friend Gene and I wore our colors. In not my smartest move ever, I parked next to a LSU tailgate party in full swing, and it took about three seconds for the sexual preferences of Arkansas women to be called into question. I chose to restrain my muscular, physical presence and practice turning the other cheek. In fact, I turned both cheeks and ran to the stadium. The Hogs got their cheeks kicked again.

In 2002, Gene, Herman, and I got up with the post-Thanksgiving shoppers at 4am and drove to Little Rock to see the game. In the greatest game I've ever seen in person, the Razorbacks pulled off a miracle in War Memorial Stadium, and I (not in my most Christian moment), enjoyed watching the humbled Tiger fans file out of the stadium.

Then, there was 2003. I don't know why I had high hopes since LSU was awesome that year and we were just so-so. I did choose to keep my Razorback t-shirt concealed under my other layers of clothes in the cold, windy weather. My great friend Roland hooked five of us up with great tickets among the 90,000-plus people gathered for the nationally televised game. We split up three and two, and Herman and I went to our seats located among the purple and gold fans. I could barely see a red shirt from our spot.

The Hogs scored first, and I concealed my huge desire to whoop and holler. I just smirked, and looked forward to a great day. Then, LSU scored. It went back and forth like that in the first quarter, with the game last tied at 17-17. Then, it quit going back and forth. Well, not really. The Razorbacks just kept going back, and the Tigers kept going forth. It ended up four thousand to seventeen or something like that. Don't let the score fool you. It wasn't really that close.

At one point, during a rare quiet moment, a loudmouth lady seated next to us said at full volume, "You guys are too quiet. What's up with you, are you not for LSU?" With all eyes on us, and decades of Razorback history weighing heavy on my heart, I slowly rose to my feet, and at the top of my lungs began chanting, "L-S-U, L-S-U, L-S-U!"

No, not really. I'm a chicken, and even a somewhat smart chicken, but I'm not a traitor. Instead, I said, "Well, not really. I'm for Arkansas, but I'm being really quiet?!" That seemed to work. They took a vote and decided not to hurt us. Instead, I just enjoyed the rest of the game with the relief of my secret being out and the strange pleasure of employing my talent at self-deprecation. Like ...

Herman: It's 3rd and 80 again, what do you think they should call?

Al: I think they should call that fumble play again. That's been our best so far.

No, It wasn't a pretty game at all. We still had a great time, and in retrospect, I think I learned at least one important lesson: No matter what side you're for, eventually everyone will find out, no matter how hard you try to conceal it.

Father,
May we choose Your team—unashamedly ...
Through Jesus,
Amen

A: LSU (30-17-2)

WINTER

Endure the winter.

The cool air of autumn goes away, replaced by the cold, bitter air of winter, but the football games do not stop. The battles simply increase in intensity. Fierce rivalries renew their passion when winter descends. The Cadets from West Point and the Midshipmen from Annapolis declare civil war. The Trojans and the Bruins battle for supremacy of the west. The eyes of Texas turn to watch A & M battle the Horns. Wolverines and Buckeyes meet up north in the bitterest weather of all.

And then come the bowl games. Pageantry yes, with beauty queens, marching bands, and extravagant floats on parade, but in the end, football teams leave everything they have on the field, including their wintry battle gear. ESPN carries all the BCS arguments, and new money-hungry corporations sneak their names on to historic games, none of which matters. Teams still play their guts out for roses and oranges, cotton and sugar.

But football does not end with the final collegiate polls, whether an obvious national champion emerges or not. Instead, the young men stop to watch while the real men battle on. Lambeau Field ices over, and Brett Favre smiles and invites someone over to play. The playoffs are set, and the inevitable attrition begins, and by the end of January, two teams full of mighty warriors remain standing to play on the biggest single night of sports of the year. Businesses pay millions just for little commercials. Famed musicians come to town just to entertain the half-time crowd. The game comes and goes. Vince Lombardi's trophy is presented.

It comes at the end of the winter. It is super. Life extinguished in a blaze of glory.

Every four years, the Olympic flame emerges for its snow-covered version of their games, too. New converts to sports like curling and luge are baptized in the icy water, and great athletes no one had ever heard of take the arctic stage. Most won't be remembered again. Some will. Some even make us believe in miracles.

In the frosty temperatures of winter, many sports fans head indoors, devoting their attention to Naismith's game. In high school gyms, hometown heroes burst through white paper run-throughs to the cheers of loyal fans, and the jeers of the town down the road. Leather basketballs unmistakably thump on hard wood, high-dollar sneakers wet down by spit squeak across the floor, whistles shriek, and unbelievably loud buzzers erupt leaving sports fans mesmerized by the sounds. When the clock runs down, and the game is close, the cheerleaders' unified yells and the crowd's fever pitch create a literal pandemonium of noise.

In the winter.

At the higher levels, the only change is (against all odds) an increased volume in it all. The Bluedevils take on the Heels. The Jayhawks meet the Sooners. The Hoosiers face the Wolverines. The Wildcats of Kentucky take it to the Bulldogs of Georgia. The Hoyas host the Huskies. Arizona heads to UCLA. The players and the coaches, they come and go, but these games never lose their intensity.

And as the old year ends and the new one claims to begin, despite the expression of the weather, we all resolve to do some things better. The cold and the bitter year that is left reminds us of all we lack, but a new year's promise gives us hope. We dream of an approaching sun.

So NASCAR fans head to Daytona to watch their favorite race.

And the tennis players turn the world upside down in Australia, confusing us all with a sunny start to another Grand Slam season.

And even the football players, in a final act of calendar treason, end up wearing leis in Honolulu, giving interviews on a tropical sideline to everyone except John Madden. He chooses to stay with us in the cold and watch, but he agrees with us as we admit: There must be hope after all. We've almost made it. Spring simply must be right around the corner.

Yes, endure the winter.

Life will change soon.

Week 40: Sid

trivia

Q: What is Fort Worth Polytechnic High School's mascot?

"Greatness is a matter, not of size, but of quality, and it is within the reach of everyone of us. Greatness lies in the faithful performance of whatever duties life places upon us and in the generous performance of the small acts of kindness that God has made possible for us. There is greatness in patient endurance; in unyielding loyalty to a goal; in resistance to the temptation to betray the best we know; in speaking up for the truth when it is assailed; in steadfast adherence to vows given and promises made."—Sidney Greenberg

I hail from Arkansas, and my home state has its share of interesting names. Possum Grape, Arkansas, is a real community, as is Oil Trough and Bald Knob. There is even a little place near my hometown affectionately known as Goobertown.

One of the towns that received the most laughs after I had left home, however, was Weiner, Arkansas. That's right, just like the hot dog. And no, Oscar Mayer is not the police chief.

Actually, one of the best basketball teams in our conference was the Weiner Cardinals. We had some "heated" games with Weiner, and I "relish" those memories (he, he, he). When you traveled to their gym, you would see a large picture on the gym wall of a cardinal driving a vehicle. The vehicle was an automotive version of a hot dog. I promise I'm telling the truth. I guess you might as well laugh at yourself, right?

There was something else you would see at a Weiner Cardinal game, including games away from their home turf. Sid. Sid was always there.

Sid was not all there mentally, but physically he was always present. His life revolved around the Weiner Cardinals, and he would not consider missing a game. In fact, stories about Sid are legendary. Sid would walk to every "away" game, at times meaning that he would walk up to fifty miles one way. He would rarely accept an offer to ride. When asked, his classic standard response was, "No, I'm in a hurry." No one knew exactly how, but Sid was always at the Cardinals' games.

As his age and legend increased, the school district convinced Sid to ride the bus with the team round-trip. Sid was in heaven. He loved the Weiner Cardinals.

I knew Sid as well as the stories. We all did. His legend preceded him.

It will succeed him as well. I thought of Sid because I saw a paper from home that told of his death. Sid passed away with cancer at age seventy. His funeral was covered in the sports section of the newspaper, and at his funeral, as suspected, many high school athletes attended.

The article mentioned several things, but one in particular made me think. The school superintendent told of several fights that occurred because of Sid over the years. Not because Sid started anything. Instead, students from other schools would make fun of Sid, and the Cardinals would stand up for their biggest fan. No one was allowed to make fun of Sid.

I have had many experiences with teenage boys. I was once one myself. And best I remember, defending a mentally challenged man has never been high on teenage boys' priority lists. It was with multiple generations of these guys, though.

The reason is obvious: Sid's innocent loyalty to the Cardinals resulted in loyalty returned.

Works the same with spiritual matters, I believe. We love because He first loved us, the Bible says. Jesus' willingness to be humiliated out of devotion to us leaves us with a similar devotion to Him. At least it should.

What I question is whether we will take up our crosses and love others in those same ways. Will we innocently love our neighbors, accepting the scorn that may come, in order that someday they may see our undying loyalty and respond in kind?

It worked in the town of Weiner, Arkansas, with a mentally challenged man named Sid. Maybe it will work where you live, too.

Father,
May our loyalty to You be expressed in our loyalty to others, and may that loyalty enable others to see what sparked it all.
In His Name,
Amen

A: The Parrots (that's right, they're known as the Poly Parrots)

Week 41: Fantasy Sports

trivia

Q: In 2002, how many people played fantasy sports on Yahoo?

"If we were willing to learn the meaning of real discipleship and actually to become disciples, the church in the West would be transformed and the resultant impact on society would be staggering."
—David Watson

I think I'm addicted.

In spite of my fondness for sports, I had little experience in the world of fantasy sports until recently. A few years back, at the low point of my contemporary sports knowledge, a friend invited me in to a fantasy basketball league. I knew just enough to be dangerous, and my dismal performance embarrassed my family name.

But I'm addicted now. Fantasy football got me hooked, and given the high cost involved (free), I suited up three teams the first time around. I even signed up for Fantasy Hockey, though I know nothing of the sport. I ended hockey season in second place. Go figure. I'd appreciate your support for the "Big Owls" wherever they may play.

When I was a kid, the old newspaper-style version of the Sporting News sported ads for a game called "Strat-o-Matic." I don't remember much about the game, except that I salivated over it, and that it was cost prohibitive for me. From what I remember, though, it was a primitive baseball version of fantasy sports leagues today. You studied the stats. You drafted your team. You competed against others, making deals along the way. And your success depended on how those guys performed on the field.

That might not have been how Strat-o-Matic worked, but that's what I remember about it. I know that from an early age, sports strategy could capture my attention like nothing else. The call was so great that from early on I wanted to be a coach.

But I'll tell you something funny. Being a coach is significantly different from Strat-o-Matic. Significantly different from fantasy sports leagues, too. It isn't too taxing to pick out a bunch of talented players, sit back and watch them perform, and ditch them when they let you down. In fact, that's fun and easy.

Coaching, on the other hand, is quite difficult.

In the real trenches, you have to teach. You have to put up with frustrating people. You have to practice the same stinking thing a thousand times, only to find your team still screws it up at game time. You have to fail in public. You have to deal with tempers and personality conflicts. No, coaching is quite different from life in the fantasy sports leagues. "Fantasy" is an apt descriptor of it all.

In spiritual matters, too.

I think most of us prefer the fantasy discipleship league. You know the league, it's where you get to pick out the Christians you want on your team, watch them perform, and ditch them when they let you down. Not much work involved at all. Fantasy discipleship, I'd call it.

Real discipleship, however, is extremely different. Repetitive teaching is necessary, along with patience. Frustrations are part of the game, as is failure. Day to day dealings with tempers and personality conflicts come with the territory as well. It's a whole different ballgame, I'm saying.

But they don't put fantasy sports leagues on pay-per-view. They don't offer multi-million dollar contracts to the best fantasy sport coaches around. Instead, they reserve all that stuff for the real game, the one with long, hard work, frustrations and failures, tempers and personality problems. Those teams that truly appreciate the end rewards.

The analogies, they do go on ....

Father,

May we get off the sofa, get out in the hot sun, and be willing to be a real part of the team.

Signed,

Your free agents

A: Over one million

Week 42: Pride 

trivia

Q: Who was Vince Lombardi's college coach, and what was his claim to fame?

"Live such good lives among the pagans that, though they accuse you of doing wrong, they may see your good deeds and glorify God on the day he visits us."—Peter

A good friend at least warned me before my move to Mississippi about the cost of car tags. Instead of personal property taxes, Mississippi gets its cash when you buy the tags for your vehicles. When a new Mississippian buys a new car, paramedics are on stand-by at the tax collector's office.

What cracks me up is that half of the state seems to have spent "extra" bucks to obtain a personalized license plate. I'm too cheap to understand, but I suppose the theory must be, "If you're already paying that much for tags anyway ...."

On my way to work one morning, I was behind a car with one of those famous personalized license plates. This one in particular read "4YOU2NV." If you're a little slow this morning, it was trying to communicate "FOR YOU TO ENVY." Make sure you're sitting down now: it was a Honda Civic. Okay, I'm sure it was a nice Honda Civic, but it was still a Honda Civic.

I'm proud of myself. I did not envy.

I'm guessing the driver is related to Vince Lombardi.

Vince Lombardi was a great coach, and it seems that he was well aware of that fact. He won six division titles, five NFL championships, and the first two Super Bowls as the legendary coach of the Green Bay Packers. They even named the Super Bowl trophy after him.

Yet once, when the coach climbed into bed with his wife, she exclaimed, "God, your feet are cold." Legend has it that Lombardi responded, "Honey, when we're alone, you can call me Vince."

If God allowed other forms of life, I'm sure humanity would be an interesting study. Some of us insist on beating ourselves up constantly while others of us make it our life's goal to truly appreciate our own greatness. And often, most people would feel it more accurate if the two groups were reversed.

There was once a young minister who was a very gifted speaker. And, as the numbers at his church began to swell, so did his head. One morning, after an inspiring sermon, one of his church members excitedly told him, "You're becoming one of the greatest expositors of this generation!" Well, on the way home, after he had squeezed his head into the family car, he couldn't resist sharing this compliment with his family. There was no response. Fishing for compliments, he went on to state, "I wonder just how many 'great expositors' there are in this generation." Unable to resist, his wife quietly said, "One less than you think, my dear."

Do you struggle with being a little too proud of yourself? Or, is your tendency more to focus on what's wrong with you? Either way is unhealthy. Why? Your focus is on you in both cases.

Sure we've got things to be proud of: made in the image of God, deemed worthy of sending God's own Son to die. Sure we've got our faults: all have sinned and fell short.

What should we concentrate on instead of those? Let's try God for a change. And I'll predict that when we do, He will remind us to turn our attention from ourselves to the good of the team.

Then, we will be ready for true success

Father,
May we stand next to You and see where we stand,
and may that humbling experience lend us a
worthwhile perspective.
Through Jesus,
Amen

A: Jim Crowley coached Lombardi at Fordham in the 1930s, and Crowley was one of Notre Dame's famed "Four Horsemen."

Week 43: The Intimidator

trivia

Q: How old was Dale Earnhardt at the time of his fatal crash?

"We talk about 'circumstances over which we have no control.' None of us have control over our circumstances, but we are responsible for the way we pilot ourselves in the midst of things as they are."—Oswald Chambers

I'll admit that I've never got into NASCAR. It grows more popular each day, so someday I may be a convert, too. But I do know that one accident out of all the racing accidents devastated racing fans the most. It happened at NASCAR's version of the Super Bowl, the Daytona 500, claiming the life of Dale Earnhardt. "The Intimidator."

I assume that all of us have had heroes, but very few of us lost our hero while he was at the pinnacle of what made him our hero in the first place, so for those that were loyal fans of Earnhardt, his accident must have been horrifying. At first, I wondered why the death of a man who raced cars for a living dominated the headlines, but NASCAR's meteoric rise in popularity had sneaked up on me. After the accident, I noticed driver's names and the circuit's logo even on carseats! And Dale Earnhardt was at the top.

Most of those who saw the replay of the crash that claimed the life of "The Intimidator" would probably agree that the accident didn't look that bad. Tony Stewart's crash on lap 174, on the other hand, was spectacular, a twenty-one-car pileup that sent Stewart's car in particular into a mid-air somersault at speeds approaching two hundred miles per hour. Yet Earnhardt's famous black #3 Chevy made one quick collision with the wall and seemed to slide harmlessly across the track. That, somehow, was fatal.

It stood to be a great day for the Earnhardt family and business. He sat in fourth place on the final lap that Sunday, battling for third, and protecting the way for the two leaders: Michael Waltrip, whose car he owned, and his own son, Dale Earnhardt, Jr. Heading into the fourth turn at 180 mph, his car seemed to brush Sterling Marlin's before sliding head first into the concrete wall, following by an impact from Ken Schrader's car.

The 195,000 spectators witnessed the crash, but had no idea the extent of the injury. Even Michael Waltrip, reveling in Victory Row over his first victory of his fifteen-year career, celebrated, "I won the Daytona 500! I can't believe it!" His mood changed drastically ninety minutes later. The fans still hanging around were stunned by the announcement made by NASCAR president, Mike Helton: "This is understandably the hardest announcement I've ever had to make. We've lost Dale Earnhardt."

Unbelievable.

As fans tried to understand, new information on safety emerged. I learned from a good friend who is a huge racing fan that he now understands that the drivers can withstand almost any crash—except a head-on contact with the wall that is. I don't think many of the fans have been able to get over it even years later. I understand vaguely that sick feeling. There is a void inside us left by the passing of every life, even someone you have never met in person, which is still very real.

As someone who meddles in the business of trying to learn lessons from the events of life, what struck me in particular about the crash of the Intimidator was this: it is often the simple looking things that do us in.

As a follower of Jesus, those spectacular, horrific events of life aren't always what drive us away from God. Actually, they often serve to drive us closer to Him. However, those innocent shortcomings, those seemingly harmless habits, those "little sins" as we like to call them: those are the most deadly.

I know I have mine to deal with. I rest assured you have yours as well. If you were a fan of Dale Earnhardt or not, I urge us all to consider what may be the greatest dangers in our lives—before it is too late.

Father,
May we understand the dangerous profession we all participate in, and may we be prepared for whatever may come.
Through Jesus,
Amen

Week 44: The Streak 

trivia

Q: What is the all-time NCAA record for all divisions for consecutive free throws?

"One hundred religious persons knit into a unity by careful organization do not constitute a church any more than eleven dead men make a football team."—A.W. Tozer

During my years coaching basketball, I had the opportunity to see the talents of Aaron Farley up close. Back then he was a little man. He stood four-feet, eleven inches, and the basketball was as big as his upper body, but that didn't keep him from draining three-pointers and knifing through the junior high trees on his way to the bucket.

There was a lot of talent around Aaron, but he always emerged as the center of attention. Certain players hated him. Others were at least a bit jealous of his talents. Every coach I came up against asked about Aaron first. Even before he topped five-feet, everyone with an eye for talent recognized his.

Aaron's talent went beyond the basketball court. In high school, he decided to take up golf. Without a lesson, and with only a couple of seasons of trying, he was the state champion in Arkansas as a junior. He repeated the accomplishment the next year. His dad always told me that he was the best young shortstop he had ever seen. The decision to give up baseball was his father's. He knew that Aaron would be drafted right out of high school, and he knew that he was too immature to see the world just yet.

He stuck with basketball. Through a series of misadventures, Aaron ended up at Harding University as a walk-on. When he met the coach, he informed him that he would soon be his best player. Aaron grew to a whopping five-feet, ten-inches, and one hundred sixty pounds by then, and he told his dad during his freshman year that he was already the second best player on the team. The coach did not agree just yet, but Aaron knew better.

As a sophomore point guard, Aaron led his team in scoring and assists and was named all-conference. As a junior, he did the same; and as a senior, he found himself in the middle of it again. This time, though, he garnered even more attention than normal.

I kept up with Aaron through Harding's basketball website, and he led his team to their best season in decades (which did not surprise me). What did surprise a lot of people were the number of free throws he continued to make. Aaron made more consecutive free throws in games (dating back to the previous season) than anyone in the history of both Divisions I and III of the NCAA. He happened to be in Division II, where the all-time record stood at ninety-eight.

Aaron's streak ended at eighty-eight. He must be human after all.

I ran across an interesting quote of Aaron's just after his streak ended. He was eight for eight on the night he missed the second of his technical free throw attempts when the ball rimmed out. The ovation lasted several minutes. He received the game ball. More importantly, at the scorer's table, he said something along the lines of, "I'd rather the scoreboard look like it does than to make every free throw." (They were slaughtering a conference rival at the time.)

We religious people need that type of attitude.

Granted, there is an individual aspect to Christianity. But there is a collective part, too. For some reason, we don't mind comparing ourselves to others, noticing our accomplishments and feats compared to the failures of others. In fact, we might be quite impressive every once in a while, at least compared to someone else. I wonder, however, if we are most concerned with the scoreboard. However you choose to see your team—a local congregation, a set of congregations in a geographic area, or the worldwide conglomeration of God's Church—the question should not so much be focused on the individual records you have amassed, but how the team is doing.

Jesus taught His disciples to pray collectively, not individually. We admire that in an athlete. When it comes down to it, we need to emulate it most.

Father,
Whatever kind of streak we may currently be on—
good or bad—may we choose to seek the good of the
team over our own accomplishments.
Through Jesus,
Amen

A: 98 (by Paul Cluxton from Northern Kentucky in the 1996-97 season)

Week 45: The Senior Bowl

trivia

Q: Which Louisiana Tech star was named MVP of the Senior Bowl in 1970?

"Christianity promises to make men free; it never promises to make them independent."—William Ralph Inge

Several men from church had a male-bonding opportunity one January. We piled in two cars, along with our winter clothing, to go to Mobile, Alabama, to watch the Senior Bowl. The Senior Bowl is an annual event that showcases top college football seniors attempting to impress the professional scouts before the draft. The pre-game hype claimed that the South squad that year boasted the greatest group of quarterbacks in Senior Bowl history. The actual game ended up with the greatest quarterbacks in history leading their team to zero points as the North won 17-0. We had fun anyway.

When we arrived, we squeezed our two cars in somebody's yard at five bucks apiece, bundled up, and walked over to the stadium. At the start of the game, the weather cooperated nicely. The blue skies, cool air, and bright sun combined to give us perfect "football weather" for the first half of the game. The play was unspectacular, but the surprising weather did not make me jealous of the fans watching at home on ESPN.

At halftime, the sun dropped behind the press box and the temperature dropped a hundred and fifty degrees (or so). I suspect all of us debated in our minds whether we should leave or not, but we waited on spectacular football that never came instead. By game's end, my feet were frozen solid and my chin was numb. You're telling me it's strange to have a numb chin. Such was my day.

Nonetheless, I picked up my chin and sauntered back to our cars where the real fun was about to begin. We discovered that our two cars, along with a soon-to-be new friend's car were blocked in by a solitary SUV. Of course, we assumed that the "blocker-inner" would be there soon. Of course, we were wrong. In fact, by the time we left ONE HOUR LATER, they still weren't there. Our exit would have to be creative.

Since it was a football game, I wish I had a chalkboard to diagram the parking situation to you. The three cars in question were completely blocked in by just one SUV. We examined every possible situation that might lead to our escape, but to no avail. We even tried to combine and lift the front (heaviest) part of the SUV and move it to the side to give us a way out, but we needed the combined offensive lines of the Senior Bowl to even stand a chance. We were stuck. So we waited ... And waited ... And waited ....

At some point, we noticed that we were not in the safest part of town and that the sun was going down. Eventually, we found our break. There was one other vehicle in the yard, a mini-van parked just to the side of our truck. These folks were MIA the whole time, too, but they arrived at the one-hour mark. With significant effort, we and our new friends helped them navigate a tight squeeze out, and with that, we had our chance.

No, we couldn't get out yet, but in a show destined to be more entertaining than the game, we combined to manually move our truck. We gathered around the tail end (the light end, by the way), flexed our frozen muscles, and after several attempts, moved the truck where we could get out. With careful driving, all three cars made their escape. Upon reflection, I think there is a lesson in there for all of us: Don't go to the Senior Bowl. You can thank me later.

Above that, though, I think we all find ourselves trapped from time to time. We may be alone, or we may be trapped along with others, but we know what it feels like to search for every possible escape and come up empty. There is nothing left for us to do but wait. And the freedom we desire can only come with help. Someone else has to make the first move. Such is the story of life.

Simply put, God always makes the first move, and the responsive efforts of humanity continue to set people free. If you feel hopelessly trapped, wait. The Bible teaches that those who "wait upon the Lord" will eventually fly to freedom. He will make the first move, and He'll have some folks there ready to do their part, too.

Father,
Teach us to wait for the help You will send.
In the name of Jesus,
Amen

A: Terry Bradshaw

Week 46: Sports Psychology 

trivia

Q: How did Yogi Berra describe the importance of psychology in baseball?

"Risk more than others think is safe. Care more than others think is wise. Dream more than others think is practical. Expect more than others think is possible."—U.S. Military Academy cadet maxim

The score was tied at ninety-three. It was overtime. There were five seconds on the clock, and my team would take the ball out-of-bounds under our own basket. The eyes of my team, as well as every other pair of eyes in the gymnasium, looked to me for the expected timeout.

I did not do as expected.

With a smile and a wink, I pointed my guys toward the floor with the instruction to run our normal out-of-bounds plays. Danny Nee of Nebraska let me in on his out-of-bounds secrets at a Nike Coaching Clinic in Chicago, and if the Falcon basketball team knew anything, they knew how to run those plays.

They confidently smiled back and rushed to their positions.

They looked at the position of Jonathan's feet to catch the play call, and when he slapped the basketball and yelled, "Break," they went to work. In the least expected place, Jeremy pinned his man on the opposite block and Jonathan threw him the ball. With a point-blank basket so obvious, the Riverside Rebel defender fouled Jeremy immediately to send him to the free-throw line.

Three seconds left now.

My opposing coach called his expected timeout to try to ice my high school junior.

I met my team halfway out on the floor, put my hand in the huddle with the quick instructions, "After Jeremy hits his free throws, set up our press like always. Don't foul, and we win." The tiny meeting broke with our customary, "1-2-3-TEAM!" chant, and my players strutted back on the floor just as the other team began their timeout.

After getting pumped up by the excited home crowd during the timeout, Jeremy calmly stepped to the line with the crowd screaming and sank his two free throws. A desperation shot by the other team, and we won.

The hero? Not Jeremy. Not me. Not even Danny Nee. It was Dr. Jeff Briggs, who didn't even know the game ever happened.

Dr. Briggs was a favorite professor of mine in college. He used to make us look through boring research journals in "Sports Psychology" class and give article reports. On one occasion, after desperately looking for something interesting, I found an article with research done on a basketball floor. The researchers used two different groups to test the effects of negative thoughts on performance. One group simply shot free throws without any words from the researchers. The others were told that people sometimes choked on the free throw line. That's all, but the latter group always performed much worse.

So a couple of years later, I as the coach expressed nothing but confidence in my players' ability to run our patented out-of-bounds plays, and the same for my athlete headed to the free throw line. They seemed confident, too. They came through in the crunch.

The Bible seems to understand this phenomenon long before sports psychologists' began their research. Paul wrote, "Do not let any unwholesome talk come out of your mouths, but only what is helpful for building others up .... " He told another group to dwell on positive things, too.

And Jesus—that original power of positive thinking guru—told his followers repeatedly to not be afraid of anything because all things are possible with God.

Maybe we should remember.

Don't shoot down the dreamers. Don't criticize the excited. In fact, with God on your side, failure shouldn't even cross our minds.

All together now ...

1-2-3 TEAM!

Let's go

A: "Baseball is 90% mental; the other half is physical."

Week 47: Dillon's Hero

trivia

Q: Who is the only father-son combination in major league history to hit back-to-back home runs in the same game?

"It is not death that a man should fear, but he should fear never beginning to live."—Marcus Aurelius

It was a quick trip to my hometown, and a quick trip back. So quick that at times I wonder if it really even happened. I made it back to the Gulf Coast around one in the morning, and during that trip, I considered some negotiations I plan to have with God. My offer is this: If I never have to see another six-year-old boy stand on his tiptoes next to his daddy's casket to say good-bye again, that will be fine with me. I have yet to figure out exactly what I have to offer in return, but I stand firm on what I'd like from God.

Scott was one of my all-time best friends. He was my best friend my senior year in high school, and not long afterwards, I helped him move to Florida to begin his life as a policeman. We stood together on Cocoa Beach to watch a nighttime rocket launch, along with a lot of other memories that only we found worth telling.

Scott faced much adversity in life. He never really knew his own father, and because of many struggles his mother faced, Scott's life alternated between living with his mom in Massachusetts and with his grandpa in Arkansas. I think Scott and I went to school together in the first, third, sixth, seventh, tenth, eleventh, and twelfth grades. He lived in New England in those alternating years.

However, Scott took on his struggles in life with everything he had. He not only took them on, but he seemed to win every time. As I rode back from the cemetery with the other pallbearers, we talked about how Scott always seemed invincible. Something that would have turned out terribly for anyone else always seemed to come out perfectly for him.

I say perfect, but no one's life is ever perfect. Scott's was not perfect when he checked out of this world that Sunday. The best part was that he had invested all of his energy in making life perfect for his kindergarten son, Dillon. Scott was known at the Kindergarten Center as "Officer Bolton" where he worked as a patrolling officer. A friend of mine informed me that Scott opened the car doors for all the little folks showing up to school each day, and that he was a real-life hero to all the kids. Dillon must have been proud to have a dad that was a hero to all the kids. Scott was Dillon's hero, his soccer coach, and his best friend.

Scott wanted Dillon to have what he never did—a real father. At the graveside yesterday, I felt so sorry for the little guy. He was just old enough to have a clue what was going on, but not old enough to catch the entire significance. Sadly, Scott wasn't there to help explain it all to him. And yet, one thought came to mind that helped the tiniest bit. Dillon has one thing that Scott never did, something no one can ever take away. He has a daddy that was a hero.

Every time he sees the video that the television station is making of the police honors, he will remember. Every time he remembers the saluting firemen that lined the road on the way to the cemetery, he will remember. And every time he looks at the flag they presented to him on that cold, confusing day, he will remember and hold on to his hero.

I told Dillon he had the coolest dad that ever lived. Without my telling him, he would have always known that anyway. Scott will miss all of the soccer games and Little Leagues and precious moments spent out in the back yard together. That makes me hurt so bad you can't even know. Yet Scott did give his son the coolest dad ever.

For a short life, that's a pretty precious gift to leave.

Father,
Bless all the little boys and girls around the world who have to grow up without their mommies and daddies. May we all learn to introduce every child to You who will never go away.
Through the hope brought by Jesus,
Amen

A: Ken Griffey, Sr. and Ken Griffey, Jr. (for the Seattle Mariners vs. the Angels on September 14, 1990)

Week 48: The N.F.L. Experience 

trivia

Q: How many times has New Orleans hosted the Super Bowl?

"I would not give one moment of heaven for all the joys and riches of the world, even if it lasted for thousands and thousands of years."—Martin Luther

Super Bowl 36 will go down as one of the most exciting Super Bowls in history, no matter what happens in the future. At present, it's finish stands as the most exciting in an already rich history. The New England Patriots, who had no business in the game in the first place, miraculously corralled the powerful Rams' offense to a measly three points throughout most of the game. I sat with a crowd in our church's "youth house" that night as the score stood 17-3 and, on one of my rare moments of correct guessing said, "They better get more than fourteen points ahead. That's nothing to this offense."

Like it was nothing, Kurt Warner and company suddenly had the game tied and headed to an obvious overtime, but this was destined to be a great Super Bowl finish. Tom Brady, a back-up simply filling in for Drew Bledsoe in the 2001 season, had only passed for 92 yards all day when the Patriots got the ball back with less than two minutes in the game and a lot of field to cover. Superman Brady, however, calmly added fifty-three yards to that total on five passes, leading the Pats down to the Ram 31-yard line with just enough time for one more play. And on the final play of the game, Adam Vinatieri became Foxboro, Massachusetts,' favorite son by splitting the uprights with a Super Bowl winning field goal. Massachusetts partied in their bitter winter.

Super Bowl host New Orleans partied, too, though that was nothing new. New Orleans is a city where mayhem is normal, and the Super Bowl Week simply whetted appetites for the upcoming Mardi Gras.

I have still never attended a Super Bowl, but I came closest to this one. I went over to the Super craziness the Friday evening before the game with my fourteen-year-old daughter and two of our friends. I had never been even close to a Super Bowl before, and we all wanted to get a taste of the hoopla. We went down near the French Quarter to an event designed just for curiosity seekers like us called the "NFL Experience."

The NFL Experience is a brilliant idea, which brings the big game to the common man. For just five bucks, you get to "experience" the sights and sensations of professional football. We did fantasy "play-by-play" broadcasts of thrilling football classics. We ran pass patterns, threw passes against simulated defenders, and caught punts. There were players there to sign autographs, MTV was preparing for their annual "rock 'n jock" game, and the biggest sports card and collectible show I had ever seen. It was a sports fan's dream comes true. I thought it was a neat concept to give everyone just a taste of what his dreams are really like.

God thinks like that, too, I believe. Thomas Boston once wrote, "Heaven is not a resting place, where men may sleep out an eternity; there they rest not day nor night, but their work is their rest and continual recreation, and toil and weariness have no place there. They rest there in God, who is the center of their souls. Here they find the completion or satisfaction of all their desires, having the full enjoyment of God and uninterrupted communion with him."

That last sentence was once a revelation to me. I believe it was C. S. Lewis, not Boston, that awakened me to that concept that Heaven is the "completion or satisfaction" of all my desires on Earth. I don't know that we consider that very often.

To be honest, most of us would prefer to stay right here because of the relationships we have and experiences the world offers. What we do not realize is that Heaven offers those very real joys in a complete form. If we really came to believe that, we would pray for Heaven to come soon. As Luther stated, we would not want to stay here—even with all the joys and riches of earth for thousands of years—if we could simply experience the fullness of Heaven for a moment.

What a game that will be.

> *Father,*
> *May we get just a taste of Your will and Your joy on earth as it is in Heaven.*
> *Come back soon.*
> *Amen*

A: A record nine times (three in Tulane Stadium, and six in the Superdome.)

Week 49: The Winter Olympics

trivia

Q: In what year were the first Olympic Winter Games held?

"Not failure, but low aim, is a crime."—James Russell Lowell

I will admit that I'm not a huge fan of the Winter Olympics. When the Games came to Salt Lake City, I'm afraid I didn't watch very closely. I did watch a large part of the opening ceremonies, and Mike Eruzione and the 1980 U.S. hockey team brought back some neat childhood memories. After that, however, I didn't keep up with it much. I heard about the figure skating controversy, and I arrogantly explained to my wife my opinion on any so-called sport that has to be rated by judges. If someone has to grade a performance, it is either an art or a school project, and not a sport in my book. One Saturday evening, however, I sat down to watch some of the Games on our fuzzy NBC channel. That night, I was introduced to "short track speed skating," and I discovered a weird, wild sport.

Short track speed skating is an odd combination of NASCAR and roller derby. Four or five guys ice skate at speeds of thirty-miles-per-hour nine times around an oval about the size of a basketball floor. They wear crash helmets because, more often than not, some guys are going down. At least that's what I witnessed in the Olympics.

That Saturday night, the top two finishers in each semi-final race were scheduled to earn a spot in the finals, and in the first semi-final race, the best three skaters all wiped out. Only two guys made it across the finish line, so they moved on. In the other semi-final, American favorite Apolo

Anton Ohno took the race and advanced into the finals. Ohno, raised by only his dad who is a hairdresser to the Hollywood stars, was a juvenile delinquent turned skating star that the announcers thought sure to win the gold medal. (I promise I'm not making this up, though I can't speak for certain for the announcers.)

Nothing is guaranteed, however, in short track speed skating.

There were five skaters in the finals (one extra skater was allowed in after the mess in the first semi). When the race began, Ohno hung toward the back of the pack. In the eighth lap, he jumped into the lead. The pack rounded the final lap, and just as Ohno headed for his gold medal, the announcers exclaimed, "Oh no!" (pun intended) as nearly the entire pack wiped out. Four skaters crashed into the wall at thirty miles per hour, and the Australian skater who was in last place crossed the finish line by himself to win the gold medal. Ohno recovered from the crash and slid across the finish line to get the silver.

The Australian celebrated his victory, and the entire world thought, "What a loser!" This guy only survived the semi-finals because the best three skaters wiped out. And in the finals, he couldn't even stay close enough to the pack to go down when they all crashed! He goes down as the best in the world?

Of course not. Sure, he has the gold medal, but everyone knows better.

I thought later about how many of us tend to emulate that Australian skater. We let everyone else go for it in life, and let them crash and burn trying to save the world. Our fear of failure is so great that we aren't really in the race, all the while hoping that somehow we will skate across the finish line in the end and get our gold medal.

Jesus did talk about the last being first and the first being last, but that actually proves my point. Standing on the medal stand, the Australian will be announced as "first," but in reality, we know he is last. The other skaters may be labeled in the record books as coming in "last," but in reality, they are the best. They are the best because they went for it. They put it all on the line. They are the real winners in everyone's book.

Robert Schuller once said, "I'd rather attempt to do something great and fail than attempt to do nothing and succeed."

Me, too.

And I believe God esteems all of us juvenile delinquents who do so more than those who hang around the back of the pack waiting for us to fail.

Father,
May we "go for it" in life—in the things that truly matter.
In the name of Jesus, who modeled this for us ...
Let it be

A: 1924

Week 50: Jarrod

trivia

Q: The highest award in baseball for sportsmanship and community activism is named after which Hall-of-Famer?

"Therefore do not worry about tomorrow for tomorrow will worry about itself. Each day has enough trouble of its own."—Jesus

Jarrod will always be one of my favorite people. He was a lot of fun. His six-foot-four, two hundred pound body, punctuated by a big goofy grin always made you think he was up to something, and as his coach and friend, I was never sure if that was good or bad. His contagious personality served as a friend magnet. He was rarely, if ever, alone.

Jarrod was a very good athlete. He ran on our state championship track team and was an All-District basketball player; he had our only dunk of the year in our record-setting 107-point game.

Jarrod also had a soft heart. His life wasn't simple, and I had the honor of talking to him heart to heart at times. One of the best things I've ever done in my life was to tell him I loved him. He said he loved me, too. Once, after he was out of high school, he even gave me a hug and said he loved me in front of one of his tough friends.

Jarrod paid attention to everyone, even those no one else noticed. It would have been so easy for someone as popular as he to ignore those considered strange by others. I look back now and wonder if he somehow related to those desperate for attention.

I'll never forget that Jarrod was the first student to know I was dating Jody. He figured it out pretty quickly when he caught us kissing in the school parking lot late one night after a game. He made sure I knew that he knew the next morning when he stuck his head into my first-period class, and without a word flashed that big goofy grin. Jarrod showed up at our house on our honeymoon, too, not realizing it. I guess he had the knack for being in the right place at the wrong time when it came to Jody and me.

On the night after Valentine's Day, 1996, Jarrod was in the wrong place at the wrong time. Jarrod and one of his friends showed up at yet another friend's house about three in the morning. They had been out doing who knows what, and they knocked on their buddy's window so they could come in and sleep a couple of hours. Their friend went to the front door carrying a gun, a bit disoriented by the ruckus at that time of night. Once his fear subsided, he motioned them in, when the gun accidentally discharged. The unintended bullet entered Jarrod just above his lip and went directly into his brain. He died shortly afterwards.

I had the honor of being a pallbearer. It was neat to see how many people loved Jarrod. I sat by Dean, his other basketball coach, and we wondered aloud if we could have done anything different that might have had him somehow in bed at three in the morning instead of in the way of an accidental bullet. I really don't think so.

I haven't mentioned that Jarrod had many faults. Don't we all. But he taught me something very important in the time I had to know him: Live each day to the fullest. I remember we were at a team camp once, and we all sat around talking in our dorm one night about the future and our purposes in life. I asked Jarrod if he ever lay in bed wondering what he would do with his life. He said, "No. When I lay in bed, I think of stuff like, 'No, I can't do that tomorrow. Yeah, maybe that's what I can do instead.'" As always, we laughed. That was just Jarrod.

As it turned out, he didn't need to think a lot about retirement plans. His life didn't last that long. I wonder why I worry so much about the distant future. Do I know how long I have left? No. I should probably be thinking a little more about today.

At Jarrod's funeral, I asked myself, "If he would have known that Valentine's Day would have been his last day on earth, I wonder if he would have done anything differently?” I doubt it. I expect he would have been with a friend at three in the morning enjoying life to the very end.

Father,
Life to the fullest. May we live it that way.
Through Jesus's promise,
May it be true

A: Roberto Clemente

Week 51: Super Bowl Hero

trivia

Q: Who was the first defensive player to be named Super Bowl MVP?

"The real tragedy of life is not in being limited to one talent, but in the failure to use the one talent."
—Edgar W. Work

Mike Jones, Super Bowl hero.

If you don't remember the game, and if you didn't watch it closely, you might not have any idea who I'm talking about. You may remember other names from Super Bowl 34 like Kurt Warner, Torry Holt, Marshall Faulk, Steve McNair, or Eddie George, but Mike Jones? In 1999, the Rams and the Titans were simply emerging as football powers. Air McNair was a new nickname to football fans, and Kurt Warner's grocery sacking stories were still novelties. The Super Bowl in early 2000 made them both stars.

Warner's MVP regular season didn't continue flawlessly through the early part of the big game, but by the third quarter, he had still led his team to a 16-0 lead. McNair, on the other hand, simply staged his legend for gritty comebacks it seemed, soon leading the Titan comeback to tie the score and bring every fan back to their couches. One play later, Warner and Torry Holt and seventy-three yards put the Rams back in the lead.

But McNair did not know how to give up. With under two minutes on the clock, the football version of his Air-ness added to his Super Bowl record rushing statistics for quarterbacks in his desperation scrambles, and completed five passes, too. But the clock kept winding down, leaving the Titan Super Bowl hopes on one play where they had to get in the end zone.

The biggest and nastiest defenders the Rams could produce simply could not bring down McNair on that final play, who at this point of the game resembled a mythical god. With one final heroic scramble, McNair found Kevin Dyson his best option available in a rub pattern across the middle, and got the ball to him.

Mike Jones, linebacker for the St. Louis Rams, assumed the Super Bowl stage. Mike Jones, in his seventh NFL season after not being drafted out of the University of Missouri, stepped up. Mike Jones, the soon-to-be Super Bowl hero, tackled Kevin Dyson on the final play of Super Bowl 34, bringing him down about a foot from that tantalizing end zone.

It was spectacular given the circumstances, but in reality Mike Jones was just doing his job. He only did what he has been doing since the first day of training camp, but to his team, it made all the difference in the world.

What about these other Super Bowl heroes: Todd Lyght and Dexter McCleon? You don't recognize them either? These were the Ram cornerbacks that were all over the "other" wide receivers that weren't open to receive a touchdown pass from Air McNair.

Just doing their job.

Team sports seem to bring out so well the importance of every individual performance. Just one person failing to do their part can spell disaster for a team. It works the same way in God's church. "...God has arranged the parts in the body, every one of them, just as he wanted them to be. If they were all one part, where would the body be?....The eye cannot say to the hand, 'I don't need you!' And the head cannot say to the feet, 'I don't need you!' On the contrary, those parts of the body that seem to be weaker are indispensable..."

You and I both have a vital position on God's team. If you don't know what it is, please find an assistant coach in your community to help you locate your place on the roster. If you do know your position, I ask you, will you come up big on the goal line in the greatest game of them all?

Father,
Thank You for allowing us to have a spot on the team. And, thank You for making it an important spot even though we know we don't deserve that honor. Please train us and motivate us and discipline us so that we come through in the crunch when souls are at stake.
Through Jesus,
Your team

A: Chuck Howley of the Dallas Cowboys in Super Bowl V. (He is also the only player to be named MVP from a losing team.)

Week 52: The Brothers Of The Barbecue 

trivia

Q: Who said, "When I was a small boy growing up in Kansas, a friend of mine and I went fishing and as we sat there in the warmth of a summer afternoon on a riverbank we talked about what we wanted to do when we grew up. I told him that I wanted to be a real major-league baseball player, a genuine professional like Honus Wagner. My friend said that he'd like to be President of the United States. Neither of us got our wish."

"Better fare hard with good men than feast it with bad."—Sir Thomas Fuller

Allow me to introduce "the Brothers of the Barbecue." Gene is our fearless leader. He didn't ask to be our leader. He's just fearless, and we follow him wherever he goes. Gene is the greatest baseball fan on the face of the earth, and despite my objections, a diehard fan of the Atlanta Braves. If time and money allow, he will drive anywhere at anytime to see a professional baseball game.

Metz is an important part of the "brothers," too. He played football against Mike Ditka in high school ("He hit me so hard—my helmet flew one way, the football went another, one shoe went another way .... ") He is a fan of the Dodgers and pretty much anything near his hometown of Pittsburgh, Pennsylvania.

The "brothers" would not be complete without Tandy. Tandy is a walking wealth of sports knowledge that roots for the Braves, but loves all things Memphis. He was a professional bowler, twice the state champion of Tennessee, with numerous perfect games under his belt. Legend has it that his best game is a game of pool, but most of his attention now is given to golf, the one game he has not been able to master.

Wayne is another valuable "brother." Wayne has been known to take in a round of golf or two in his day as well. In fact, Wayne hosted a golf outing of the "brotherhood" one weekend, complete with a gumbo lunch at his house afterwards. Wayne roots for the Texas Rangers, which took a hit when they lost his favorite player, Rafael Palmeiro. He also pulls for those LSU Tigers.

DeJon is an LSU nut as well. His college career at Texas Tech allows him two college teams, but LSU has his heart. Based on a cool Ryne Sandberg story from his childhood, DeJon is a longsuffering Chicago Cubs fan as well. He still speaks to me even thought I'm of the rival Redbird persuasion.

Hal is another original member of the "brothers." Hal was our old (veteran, not old) softball pitcher, a man that saved our team from my pitching over several seasons. He is also another golf enthusiast. He has my respect, since he is an Arkansas Razorback alumni and a Hog fan through and through.

Ron is a "brother" from the start. Ron is yet another fan of the Atlanta Braves. He traveled from the Gulf Coast to his home state of Michigan a few years back with Gene, just so they could catch a game at Tiger Stadium before they shut it down. Ron pays more attention to the Big 10 than the rest of us SEC guys, rooting for the Big Blue.

Along with me, Herman is a co-founder of the "brothers of the barbecue." Herman is a fan of the Miami Hurricane football program, Duke Bluedevil basketball, the Atlanta Braves, and in his only good choice, a longsuffering Dallas Cowboys fan. Herman was a football lineman in high school and follows sports even more than I do.

Then, there's me. I guess it was my idea originally. Some ladies from church started a group called the "Sisters of the Skillet." I joked about it, saying that we ought to come up with a group called, "Brothers of the Barbecue." So we did. We come up with excuses to get together and share our enjoyment of sports with one another.

We've gone to Hattiesburg to watch college football and try weakly to get on ESPN. We went to Mobile to the Senior Bowl. We've made road trips to Atlanta and Houston, both for major league baseball. We have a great time together. There are other "brothers" out there, too, and I suspect there will be even more to come. I, for one, need our little group. More than even I realize.

In a generation when Promise Keepers hit it big, and in a society where sports bars stay full and poker buddies hide out, I need a group of guys with which to just plain have fun and share life, too. There's some informal counseling along the way, and a lot of laughter. Above all, though, there are some pretty great memories being formed.

Long live the "Brothers of the Barbecue." May you have some good friends, too.

Father,
Even Jesus traveled with some buddies, didn't He?
Thank You for that gift.
Through Him,
Amen

A: Dwight D. Eisenhower

Afterword

The Personal Testimony of Baseball Hall-of-Famer, George Kell

I was raised in a Christian home along with two brothers, and a loving mother and father. My father was an outstanding semi-pro player who could have gone a long ways in pro ball, but he chose not to leave his family behind as those of us who made a career of baseball. When I was growing up, we were in Sunday School and Church every Sunday—and sometime too much during the week I thought. But our father encouraged our baseball playing.

The first pastor I can remember at the small Swifton Methodist Church was Paul V. Galloway, who was in his first year out of the School of Divinity at Yale University. He loved to play baseball, so he and my dad mixed well. They both loved the church and loved to play baseball. My father was the manager of the local team, and Reverend Galloway played first base—even on Sunday. This was a little too much for some of his flock, so at the end of one year he left. But like a lot of ball players, it did not diminish his love for God and the ministry. His ministry proved to be long and successful. When I was inducted into the Hall of Fame in 1983, he watched it on television. He wrote me a note that said, "Your talk was humorous, honest, and reflected your Christian raising."

My father was in a nursing home in Newport, Arkansas, at the time of my induction. My mother had died eight years earlier. I had bought an automobile agency in Newport just so I could visit my father most every day. I asked my brother, Skeeter, to come to Newport and sit with dad while they watched the Induction Ceremony. Skeeter called me that night at Cooperstown, and I asked him how dad liked it. He said he liked it fine, but he started to cry when I told the story I had told many times before. I told that huge crowd and the television audience that my father raised "three" sons, convinced they would all be major league ballplayers, if not "Hall of Famers." I told them he might have been right, too. Skeeter played two years for the Philadelphia A's in addition to my career, but his middle son was killed as a pilot in Germany in World War II. I had to pause to get myself under control at that point of my talk, but I heard a booming voice way back in the crowd yell, "He was right!" I think that booming voice saved me at that moment. It told me that people do care—even about people they do not know.

I played fourteen years in the major leagues, then after one year on the CBS Game of the Week with Dizzy Dean and Buddy Blattner, I went to Detroit where I did the play-by-play on the Tigers television games for thirty-seven years. I retired to my home in Swifton, Arkansas, after the 1996 season.

Life has been good to me. I buried my mother and father here in Swifton, and then in 1991 my wife of fifty years was diagnosed with terminal cancer. Eventually, I had to bury her as well. I married again in 1994 to a lovely lady who is younger than me, but she understood she might have to take care of me someday. Our house burned in 2001, and I was home alone. I was lucky to survive with the aid of a big fireman.

I have attended the same church for eighty-two years here in Swifton. I've been a Sunday School teacher and the lay leader of the finance committee, but it almost came to a screeching halt for me about a year ago. I got up to speak to the area Methodist Men, and after a couple of minutes, I could not read my notes or even put the words together. My wife took me to a neurosurgeon, and after one day of tests, he said I had too much fluid on the brain. He drilled a hole in my scalp, put a small tube into the hole under the skin all the way to my abdomen with a magnet under my scalp that tells them ever so often if I'm getting the proper amount of fluid off.

On August 23rd of 2004, the people of this great little town gave me a birthday party at the Civic Center to honor my 82nd birthday. Wal-Mart donated some four hundred baseballs. They sold them for five dollars apiece. I signed them all, and we gave the money to the Methodist Church and the Fire Department who saved my life.

I visited a friend in the hospital today. He told me, "George, I might not make it, but all we can do is go meet the Lord and say, 'Here I am. I've done the best I can do.' He'll understand."

Amen.

Sincerely,

George Kell

December, 2004

Resources

A few illustrations and most of the quotes in this book come courtesy of the QuickVerse software package produced by Parsons Technology in Hiawatha, Iowa (www.quickverse.com.) In particular, *Bible Illustrator* and *Draper's Book of Quotations for the Christian World* (composed by Edythe Draper and published by Tyndale House) were most useful.

The second source of quotes that I mined for gems was *Quotations for Public Speakers: A Historical, Literary, and Political Anthology*, edited by Robert G. Torricelli: Rutgers University Press, New Brunswick, New Jersey, 2001.

A third source of quotes, of course, was the wonderful World Wide Web:

Roger Hornsby:
www.brainyquote.com/quotes/quotes/r/rogershorn104218.html

Wilt Chamberlain:
www.brainyquote.com/quotes/quotes/w/wiltchambe100538.html

Wes Westrum:
www.brainyquote.com/quotes/quotes/w/weswestrum100522.html

Tommy Lasorda:
www.brainyquote.com/quotes/quotes/t/tommylasor126566.html

Rick Reilly:
sportsillustrated.cnn.com/inside_game/rick_reilly/news/2003/05/20/life_of_reilly0519/

Ty Cobb:
www.baseball-almanac.com/quotes/quocobb.shtml

Joseph Lieberman:
www.10ktruth.com/the_quotes/baseball.htm

Leo Durocher & Knute Rockne:
members.tripod.com/~cldj23/1quotes4.html

General George S. Patton:
www.usmilitaryknives.com/patton's_speech.htm

The Joe Dimaggio quote (from a George Will article):
www.polkonline.com/stories/031199/opi_dimaggio.shtml

The Clutch Hitter myth (though I can't locate the original article):
www-math.bgsu.edu/~grabine/fullclutch.txt

George Will:
www.brainyquote.com/quotes/quotes/g/georgefwi135815.html

The Jonesboro Sun:
jbs.mynewroads.com/archivedstory.asp?ID=975

Dale Earnhardt tragedy:
www.racelinecentral.com/thestory1.html

Aaron Farley:
www.harding.edu

I also referred to two books that deserve mention:

The Screwtape Letters, by C. S. Lewis. Touchstone, New York, 1996.

Life's Little Instruction Book, by H. Jackson Brown. Thomas Nelson Publishers, Nashville, 2000.

Finally, all of the trivia questions in the book came courtesy of the aforementioned World Wide Web. I trust their accuracy, though the facts may not always hold up in a court of law. In case you take issue with a trivia answer, you can locate my sources in order in the following locations:

www.azcentral.com/news/articles/0707spring07.html
www.canoe.com/StatsPGA/BC-PGA-LGNS-MASTREC-R.html
www.ncaasports.com/basketball/mens/story/6254422
sportsillustrated.cnn.com/statitudes/news/2001/03/30/openingday_btn/
www.angelfire.com/electronic/ultramentor/records_running.html
www.washingtonpost.com/wp-srv/sports/longterm/memories/final4/articles/players.htm
shoeless.myclassics.com/trivia.shtml
www.scigolf.com/scigolf/19th/aces.htm

www.undelete.org/woa/woa12-21.html

www.cosmicbaseball.com/bnr.html#menu

www.time.com/time/time100/heroes/profile/hillary_norgay01.html

en.wikipedia.org/wiki/Steve_Kerr

wso.williams.edu:8000/~jkossuth/cobb/faq.htm

www.hotspotfishing.com/records/fish-records-Eel.asp

www.baseball-almanac.com/players/player.php?p=aingeda01

www.grmcf.com/flagstick/mygame.htm

www.pawsox.com/team/longest_game

www.specialolympics.org/Special+Olympics+Public+Website/English/About_Us/History

www.historicbaseball.com/fea/baseballbroadcasts.html

www.bellathletics.com/eba_new.htm

www.metrolyrics.com/lyrics/58018/Simon_And_Garfunkel/Mrs_Robinson

www.assassinations.net

www.sportingnews.com/archives/baseball/94640.html

www.drblank.com/slaw1.htm

sportsillustrated.cnn.com/baseball/news/2002/06/18/buck_obit_ap/

www.askmen.com/men/sports/40_lance_armstrong.html

www.dartmouth.edu/~frommer/baseball2.htm

encarta.msn.com/text_761568314__1/Softball.html

www.baseballlibrary.com/baseballlibrary/ballplayers/W/Williams_Ted.stm

www.71originaltitans.com/locker.html#State

www.volleyball.org/rules/basic_rules.html

www.ymca.net/about/cont/history.htm

www.ncaasports.com/crosscountry/mens/story/6813165

www.americansportsdata.com/sports_injury1.asp

www.nba.com/history/players/reed_bio.html

www.bctenpinfed.com/ctfconmar04.htm

www.baseballlibrary.com/baseballlibrary/ballplayers/T/Terry_Ralph.stm

www.nays.org

www.mcubed.net/ncaaf/series/series.htm

www.texasmascots.com/byschool.html

fantasysports.yahoo.com

www.und.com/trads/horse.html
www.obits.com/earnhardtdale.html
www.collegesportingnews.com/article.asp?articleid=40164
espn.go.com/classic/biography/s/Bradshaw_Terry.html
www.quotedb.com/quotes/1310
www.factmonster.com/spot/fatherathletes.html
www.absolutebrady.com/Archive/GameDay2003.html
www.infoplease.com/ipsa/A0115111.html
www.robertoclemente21.com/RCMOTY/rcmoty.html
www.superbowl.com/history/mvps/game/sbv
www.brainyquote.com/quotes/quotes/d/dwightdei145976.html

About the author

Al Sturgeon's lifelong dream was to be a coach. He accomplished that dream at the high school level, coaching basketball, volleyball, track and cross-country. He was even fortunate enough to capture a couple of state championships in his brief career with the Crowley's Ridge Academy Falcons.

Later, however, he became the preaching minister at the Ocean Springs Church of Christ in Ocean Springs, Mississippi. Al may be a bit delusional, but he still believes he is a coach—just with a different type of team.

Along the way, he started writing. He has published *The Fighting Never Stops: The Story of Jim McVeay*, along with several articles for magazines and Internet sites.

He lives in Ocean Springs with his beautiful wife, Jody, and two gorgeous daughters, Erica and Hillary.